The Responsive Web

The Responsive Web

MATTHEW CARVER

MANNING

SHELTER ISLAND

For online information and ordering of this and other Manning books, please visit
www.manning.com. The publisher offers discounts on this book when ordered in quantity.
For more information, please contact

> Special Sales Department
> Manning Publications Co.
> 20 Baldwin Road
> PO Box 261
> Shelter Island, NY 11964
> Email: orders@manning.com

Manning Publications Co.	Development editor:	Cynthia Kane
20 Baldwin Road	Technical development editor:	Roberto Alarcon
PO Box 261	Technical proofreader:	Valentin Crettaz
Shelter Island, NY 11964	Copyeditor:	Andy Carroll
	Proofreader:	Melody Dolab
	Typesetter:	Marija Tudor
	Cover designer:	Leslie Haimes

ISBN: 9781617291241
Printed in the United States of America
1 2 3 4 5 6 7 8 9 10 – MAL – 19 18 17 16 15 14

brief contents

contents

preface

In May 2010 I read an article on the A List Apart website. If you picked up this book, it's likely that you know the article I'm talking about. You've probably read it and heard it quoted, picked apart, debated, and discussed. Now, nearly four years later, that article is the basis of one of the biggest movements on the web since the web standards movement of the late 90s.

When Ethan Marcotte's article, "Responsive Web Design,"[1] was published, I was still new to web development, having just started a job at my first web production agency. It had been a few months since I had bought my first iPhone and I had just started coding sites for mobile and including mobile stylesheets in my projects. I was struggling to find a good solution to mobile web development, like many developers at the time.

The iPhone changed everything and was quickly becoming my favorite way of browsing the web, but websites looked like garbage on it. Ethan's article came as a revelation—and a relief. It provided a clear path to solving a huge and immediate problem in my development workflow, and by June 2010 I started including media queries in all of my work. Responsive web design gave me something new and exciting to add to my projects and thoroughly solved the problem of mobile web design.

Beyond the technological challenges, responsive web design introduced me to a new way of working. Responsive design needs a collaborative workflow that requires equal input from both visual designer and developer. This is what excited me. Having

---

[1] http://alistapart.com/article/responsive-web-design.

been on both the design and development sides of the web, I'd always felt that harmony between both sides is the key to creating incredible digital experiences. This became the part of responsive design that stuck with me: the need for creativity in code and for design to be translated into front-end development early on.

I have this habit: whenever I find something interesting, I want to tell everyone about it. If you've ever spent more than a few minutes in my company you've probably heard me rant about any number of nerdy topics. Just try to bring up comic books, baseball, or whiskey and buckle up for some opinionated rambling. Responsive web design was no different. I told everyone I could about it and eventually had the privilege of talking about the subject at web conferences.

With this book I get to completely indulge my nerdy habit. The book represents an unboxing of my passion for what I see as a huge step in the maturity of the web. I believe the web to be one of the most important inventions in human history. The sharing of information among people is important for both inventiveness and creativity, and the web facilitates this sharing of ideas and information better than any medium in human history.

Hopefully this book will help you gain a new understanding of responsive web design. My goal was that the book would not only encourage you to start implementing responsive design, but also give you tools and language to facilitate collaboration between designers and developers. This book should facilitate the understanding you need to be part of building a new, device-agnostic web.

acknowledgments

This book has been the combined work of a team of extraordinary collaborators. Thanks to these people I've been able to do something I never thought myself capable of. I want to take this opportunity to thank these people from the absolute bottom of my heart. First, I'd like to thank Brandon Satrom and the team who made the HTML5.tx conference possible. Without that first opportunity to share my passion on a public platform, this book would have never been possible. I'd like to thank John Tornow and Randy Bradshaw, who provided me the mentorship and encouragement I needed early in my career to foster my ambition and lead me to this. I would also like to thank Chris Williams, Brooks Oakley, Justin Tabor, James Henningson, Brian Linder, and Cory Hudson for their support, encouragement, advice, and genius.

The work of writing this book hasn't been easy, especially for my collaborators at Manning. The team at Manning has been an absolute joy to work with. During the writing of this book, my life has been an adventure and through it all, the team at Manning has been fundamental in making this book possible. First, I have to thank my development editor Cynthia Kane for her guidance, patience, direction, and counsel. Cynthia went above and beyond the call of duty, time and time again, to help transform my work into something special and I will never forget the hard work she put in to help me do something I never could have imagined. I'd like to thank Roberto Alarcon for his contribution to my writing, and Andy Carroll for his copyediting and for catching a near-embarrassing level of grammatical errors and typos. I would like to thank Valentin Crettaz for his thorough work as technical proofreader; his advice and commentary were invaluable. And I would like to thank Kevin Sullivan for his work on making all the images in this book look their absolute best.

Special thanks to the following reviewers who read the manuscript at various stages of its development and who provided feedback that resulted in a much better book: Adam Murray, Benoît Benedetti, Brian Bush, Bruno Sonnino, Christopher Weiss, Daniele Midi, David Landau, Dr. Martin Beer, Gary Kirrene, Gregor Zurowski, James Bisiar, Jeff Smith, Joel Kotarski, John D. Lewis, Mike Donahue, Nikolaos Kaintantzis, Sebastian Felling, and Sergio Arbeo.

Finally, I would like to thank my wife, Alex. She's been the backbone of my life and my pillar of strength for the last six years. Without her love and support I don't know where I would be today. She encouraged me when I was starting out as a lowly free-lance web designer, building sites at night and waiting tables in the day to make ends meet. She gave me the confidence to pursue my first serious job as a web developer and was there for me when times got tough. She listened to me ramble about web design for hundreds of hours and helped me consolidate my thoughts so I could write this book. She even helped edit my first few blog posts on responsive web design. I'm the luckiest man in the world to know her. Alex, you're the love of my life.

about this book

Responsive web design is a technique of designing websites that scale for various browsers, including mobile, tablet, and desktop. It's made possible through CSS3 Media queries and offers developers the opportunity to design a site once for multiple devices. While the technique is seemingly simple, the practice itself involves several challenges.

In this book we'll discuss topics related to the practice of responsive web design that will not only give developers the opportunity to sharpen their technical skills, but will also teach designers how to design for this technique. The goal of this book is to not just present the technical challenges, but to elaborate on the design and collaborative challenges that a team faces when embracing responsive web design.

This book is not simply a manual full of step-by-step "how-to" examples. It includes insights for designers and developers into the reasoning behind the practical components of responsive web design, as well as associated tips. Each chapter is not only followed with a summary, but also includes discussion points for internal reflection or conversation starters between designer and developer. My hope is that this book is read among a team and sparks your imagination and strengthens your conversation around responsive web design. Web design is a team sport and hopefully this book will serve as a coach for your team as you delve into this new practice.

Roadmap

This book has nine chapters divided into three parts, and two appendixes, one of which is available online only.

- Chapter 1 gives an overview of how to work on a responsive website as a team. It introduces some core concepts and history of the practice.
- Chapter 2 focuses on designing for mobile screens and some of the challenges facing designers creating for smaller device screens.
- Chapter 3 introduces style tiles, a mood-board-like deliverable for articulating design style without providing layout.
- Chapter 4 gives an outline of responsive design patterns. It introduces the concept of a design pattern and gives a few examples of solving common design and layout problems in responsive design.
- Chapter 5 covers responsive layouts, focusing on grid systems and adapting page layouts through screen size changes.
- Chapter 6 starts the discussion of the challenges of responsive content. In this chapter you'll find information about how content can adapt to changing screens.
- Chapter 7 offers some insights into CSS3, specifically around adding visual graphics and style to a responsive page. It covers responsive images and video, as well as some tips and tricks about creating pages that take full advantage of CSS to scale a sites design.
- Chapter 8 introduces Modernizr, a fundamental tool for cross-browser compatibility and mobile asset optimization. You'll learn how to use Modernizr to improve site performance and effectively ensure cross-browser and cross-device compatibility.
- Chapter 9 teaches some tips for responsive testing and gives an explanation of web inspector tools so you can effectively optimize your websites.
- Appendix A "Context-aware design" is included in the book. Appendix B "Foundations" is available online at www.manning.com/The ResponsiveWeb.

Who should read this book?

The Responsive Web is a book for both sides of the front-end development coin. It's intent is to satisfy the questions posed by both designer and developer, while inspiring curiosity about the future of the web and confidence in the reader's ability. Anyone involved in a web design project can benefit from reading this book: designer, developer, or even manager.

A basic understanding of HTML and CSS will help during the development portions of this book. Ideally the reader of this book would have basic understanding of the core concepts and processes involved in web design and development. Being a coder isn't required and much of the book covers nontechnical strategy and advice, but some familiarity with basic HTML will provide a richer experience for all readers.

If you have any degree of interest in building, designing, or collaborating with teams that build responsive websites, this book is absolutely for you. It will provide substantial background to all areas of responsive web development.

Code conventions and downloads

All source code in listings or in text is presented in a fixed-width font like this to separate it from ordinary text. Code annotations accompany many of the listings, highlighting important concepts.

Inside the book you will find multiple references to source code that illustrates design and development principles. All source code for this book is available for download from the publisher's website at manning.com/TheResponsiveWeb. The source code is provided in HTML, CSS, and JavaScript. The jQuery library is used in most of the JavaScript examples. There are a few references to remotely hosted libraries, such as jQuery, that require an internet connection, but in most instances the code will function locally. The book provides instructions about the location of related source code. Most code for *The Responsive Web* is brief and lightweight, with few dependencies.

author online

The purchase of *The Responsive Web* includes free access to a private web forum run by Manning Publications, where you can make comments about the book, ask technical questions, and receive help from the author and from other users. To access the forum and subscribe to it, point your web browser to www.manning.com/ TheResponsiveWeb. This page provides information on how to get on the forum once you're registered, what kind of help is available, and the rules of conduct on the forum.

Manning's commitment to our readers is to provide a venue where a meaningful dialogue between individual readers and between readers and the author can take place. It is not a commitment to any specific amount of participation on the part of the author, whose contribution to the forum remains voluntary (and unpaid). We suggest you try asking the author some challenging questions lest his interest stray!

The Author Online forum and the archives of previous discussions will be accessible from the publisher's website as long as the book is in print.

about the author

Matthew Carver is a technologist, speaker, writer, and consultant who advocates for creative collaboration between design and technology. An early adopter of responsive web design, he's worked with clients such as American Airlines, Dallas Morning News, Chobani, Home Depot, and Google to bring innovative digital projects to life. Matthew cut his teeth in Dallas, Texas, with the digital arm of The Richards Group and now lives and works in New York City where he partners with digital agencies and start-ups to put great ideas online. He can be found online at MatthewCarver.com or on Twitter at @matthew_carver.

Part 1

The responsive way

Responsive web design dramatically changes what we build. It's a fundamental redefinition of our online output, and it requires us to take into consideration every point in the web design and development workflow.

In the first chapter of this book you'll learn to work responsively. Right off the bat, I'm going to give you all the basic information you need to get started with responsive web design. This will give you a sense of what responsive web design entails, and also how it's different from traditional web design.

In chapter 2 we'll talk about designing for mobile first. Here we'll start to cover the challenges of designing a website, keeping its mobile version in mind first. This will round out your introduction to responsive web design and give you the background you need to start building responsive websites.

Learning to work responsively

1

This chapter covers

- An overview of a responsive workflow
- Using a prototype to communicate responsive design
- Building a simple responsive website

As the web has evolved, we've learned new tactics. We've established new ways of working and added them to our older ways. Responsive web design has given us a whole new set of skills to add to our workflow. But before we can start discussing those skills, we need to answer a simple question. What exactly is "the responsive web"?

Remember when people called the internet the "information superhighway"? It sounds cheesy now, but imagine that "superhighway." Right now it's full of people in sports cars, 18-wheelers, bicycles, family sedans, racecars, and pickup trucks. Some travel at hundreds of miles an hour; others go at a snail's pace. Some legs of the highway have bike lanes, sedan lanes, and fast lanes, as illustrated in figure 1.1.

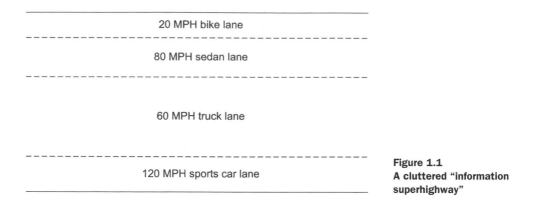

Figure 1.1
A cluttered "information superhighway"

Every once in a while, a traveler gets confused, and a sports car ends up in the bike lane, and a bike ends up in the sedan lane.

Just as the Department of Transportation created traffic standards, so the responsive web strives to standardize development patterns to accommodate users with screens of all sizes. For the last decade or so, web design and development has stayed in a fairly tight window. Websites have generally been accessed by desktop computers and laptops. Bandwidth and screen resolutions have stabilized, and most users have engaged websites with a traditional mouse and keyboard. These expectations gave us an anticipated standard, and we played within the confines of our sandbox.

With the rise of handheld and tablet devices, web design and development is undergoing a phase of rapid and painful growth. Mobile websites are nothing new—mobile-optimized websites have been around for over a decade. The problem lies in the architecture of these mobile sites.

Ethan Marcotte (coauthor of *Handcrafted CSS* and *Designing with Web Standards, Third Edition*)[1] wrote an article for the online magazine *A List Apart* called "Responsive Web Design" that proposed a new technique for designing web pages to accommodate the needs of users with screens of all sizes, from mobile to desktop (http://mng.bz/pOIb). Marcotte expanded the article into one of the most groundbreaking books in the history of web design, *Responsive Web Design* (A Book Apart, 2011). Marcotte's book struck a resonating chord among designers and developers worldwide, and the principles he described sparked a revolution.

This book is written to transform your process, whether you're a designer, developer, or both, or if you support or manage designers or developers. This book exists to give you the tools you need to understand this new way of creating according to the rules of the responsive web. With this book, you'll learn how to work with the limited screen real estate of small-screen devices, such as smartphones. We'll cover the

---

[1] Dan Cederholm and Ethan Marcotte, *Handcrafted CSS* (New Riders, 2009); Jeffrey Zeldman and Ethan Marcotte, *Designing with Web Standards, Third Edition* (New Riders, 2009).

concepts and technologies that are crucial to responsive web design and equip you with the knowledge you need to be a part of the responsive web.

This chapter serves as a quick introduction to the responsive web and its core concepts and gives you a base on which to get started. Once we get through the basic concepts, you'll build your first responsive site!

Designer/developer insights

In this book, the lines between what's considered "design" and what's considered "development" are blurred. Occasionally, these roles are occupied by one person, and other times multiple people take on these responsibilities. Either way, the responsive web requires harmony between the two skillsets.

The goal of this book is to teach designers and developers not only the practices and executions that will produce successful responsive websites, but also how to communicate and collaborate more efficiently. Responsive design is truly successful when you focus on how you work as well as what you produce.

There are some sections in this book that dive deeply into teaching design principles, and other parts talk specifically about skillsets important to developers. Knowledge of both the design and development skills involved in responsive design is important to a balanced education on the topic. Be sure to look for sidebars like this one to draw out those connections and provide discipline-specific insights.

1.1 Meet the responsive web

I know you may be eager to start building your first responsive site, but before we do, I want to make sure you have the basics under your belt. In this section, I'll let you in on what the responsive web really is and what its key features are. Once you're through with this quick introduction, you'll be ready to start building.

1.1.1 What is the responsive web?

In order to move forward, we need to set a few ground rules about what, exactly, we mean by *the responsive web*:

- A responsive site, like the one shown in figure 1.2, is one that uses a single URL for mobile, tablet, and desktop sites. With about 15%[2] of traffic (and more all the time) coming from mobile devices, and an increasing number of tablets and smartphones on the market, these devices are a crucial segment of all web traffic.
- Because responsive web design relies on media queries to adjust to page width, the responsive web requires CSS3 support and updating to HTML5.

---

[2] Mary Meeker and Liang Wu, "Internet Trends D11 Conference" (May 29, 2011), https://kpcb.com/file/kpcb-internet-trends-2013.

Figure 1.2   An example of how a responsive website behaves for a single URL (http://mng.bz/ vTVT). The "Activism" section of the 2013 Webby Awards can be accessed by multiple devices with different hardware properties.

- A responsive site strives for consistency across devices. By using a single URL, you ensure that all inbound links to your site serve consistent content.
- A responsive site delivers faster and heightens user experience. By developing mobile sites first, an emphasis is placed on efficiency.
- A responsive site is future-friendly. Every site will eventually need to be optimized for new technology, but by building responsively, you ensure that optimization won't entail a full site redesign.

If you've been involved in designing or developing a website, you probably have a standard workflow. You have tools you use in certain ways to construct your work. In many cases, building a responsive site requires making adjustments to these tools and using entirely new tools.

Traditional web development takes a waterfall approach. The project follows a sequence, typically along the lines of figure 1.3.

The waterfall approach becomes inefficient and costly if the team needs to consider variations on a project. Also, what if there are inconsistencies or performance

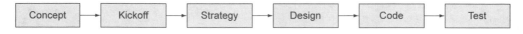

Figure 1.3   Commonly called the "waterfall method," each phase in this process involves creating and passing a deliverable to the next person in the workflow.

issues when you get to development? Suddenly the entire project has to be changed, and even potentially rebuilt.

The responsive web is about adaptation. With responsive web design, teams work closely together to build a site. Instead of passing off deliverables along the "website assembly line," teams iterate and improve upon each other's work (figure 1.4).

In the traditional pixel-perfect web, the emphasis was on re-creating the layout work from the art/design department, but in this approach, the emphasis is on adapting. Using the standard pixel widths and font sizes won't do anymore. We need something a little more fluid.

By focusing on adapting and giving the site a fluid layout, your site stands to gain several things:

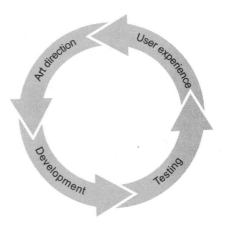

Figure 1.4   In this new, more agile approach, user experience and development happen iteratively. Deliverables are passed along and reviewed in an iterative cycle.

- *A layout that adapts to variations in screen-size technology*—If a new web-enabled product hits the market with an uncommon screen, then you're already prepared for it.
- *A faster site*—By optimizing for mobile first, you prioritize load times from the beginning of development. Faster sites are always better.
- *Simpler browser-specific development*—Cross-browser layout issues can actually be easier to resolve with fluid CSS.

1.1.2   Key features

The responsive web couldn't exist as it is without two components: media queries and breakpoints. These features are what create cross-browser responsiveness and give websites the ability to adapt to the user's screen.

MEDIA QUERIES

A media query is a type of CSS rule that limits a style's scope based on factors defined by the query. Each media query specifies a media type and a set of expressions that are checked by the browser. Possible media types include screen for digital screens, print for printed pages, and all for all media types. Expressions are more detailed and include instructions such as max-width or orientation.

Media queries come from a specification in the 2001 working draft of the W3C CSS3 proposal,[3] which presented a solution to the problem of offering various CSS rules depending on browser size and device screen size. Media queries are an

---

[3]   W3C, "Introduction to CSS3," W3C Working Draft, 23 May 2001, www.w3.org/TR/2001/WD-css3-roadmap-20010523/.

ingenious solution, and they're the life and spirit of the responsive web. They can be used to deliver CSS rules based on a number of factors, including screen resolution, orientation, and even color index. Without them, mobile web development would be in a really tight spot.

The media query is simple and looks something like this:

@media initiates the query, and then you can start declaring what media you'd like to target or your media type. In this case, the media type is digital screens.

```
@media screen {
  p{ font-family: sans-serif; }
}
```

Between the brackets you can apply your usual CSS, but it will only affect browsers on digital screens in this case.

This line in a stylesheet will tell the browser to give paragraph tags the `font-family` of `sans-serif`, but only on screens. It won't give the style to printed pages or handhelds that recognize themselves with the media type *handheld*.

Now imagine something like this:

```
@media handheld{
  p{ font-family: sans-serif; }
}
```

With that line, you're now targeting any user on a device that identifies itself as handheld. In practice, when your site targets modern and popular devices, this particular media query is fairly useless, because most of the device manufacturers define their devices with the *screen* media type (iOS, Android, even the Kindle experimental browser).

A media query can also be used to serve a relevant CSS file based on the criteria laid out in the media query in a `<link>` tag. In this format, a media query is served within the head tag at the very top of a web page, and looks like this:

```
<link rel="stylesheet" type="text/css" media="handheld" href="sans-
    serif.css">
```

This example allows you to load this stylesheet only for browsers that identify themselves as being `handheld`.

The biggest difference between these two methods is that serving a separate stylesheet for mobile requires additional HTTP requests for each stylesheet. The browser will only load the stylesheets that pass the media query, and this can be used strategically to limit the total amount of CSS on a page.

The key to using media queries in responsive design lies in their ability to serve CSS based on viewport width, which is the width of the browser window. These media queries are what are called *expressions*, and they're the parameters that the browser checks.

Information a device relays to a server includes the browser agent, the resolution of the device being used, and the size of the window viewing the page. In the responsive web, it's important to note these factors and to understand their differences. Using media queries, you can serve CSS based on either viewport width or device width.

To apply CSS based on a viewport with a width of 400 pixels or less, you'd use a media query like this:

```
@media (max-width: 400px) { ... }
```

Alternatively, if you needed to target only devices whose width is 400 pixels or less, you could change your expression to something like this:

```
@media (max-device-width: 400px) { ... }
```

It's important to note the differences between the two, because in some cases you might wish to serve the smaller-size rules to a browser window that's been slimmed down, to prevent the appearance of a horizontal scrollbar or create a better user experience. You might wish to target only small-screen devices if you'd prefer desktop users to be given the full-screen version of a site, regardless of window size.

Another helpful distinction that you'll want to be aware of is the difference between a `min-width` and a `max-width` media query. `@media (max-width :400px){...}` targets a browser with a width of 400 pixels or less, whereas `@media(min-width:400px){...}` targets a browser with a width of 400 pixels or more. With `max-width`, the rules affect every viewport below the set width, but `min-width` affects everything *over* the viewport width specified.

So how does one decide when to use a media query? That brings us to our next topic...

BREAKPOINTS

The goal of responsive design is to avoid what Ethan Marcotte refers to as the "zero sum game" of redesigning a website for every possible device and viewport.[4] To avoid this, you need to identify boundaries for where you'll alter your layout to fit the needs of the changing context. As the site you're working on goes from a mobile device width to a desktop width, at what point does it change or "break"?

This is what's called a *breakpoint* in responsive design. Breakpoints are the points at which new rules are served to the responsive site. In figure 1.5 you can see an example of three potential breakpoints in a page.

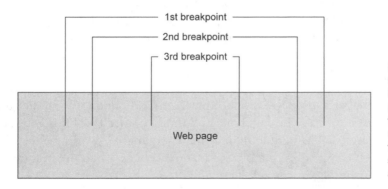

Figure 1.5 A visual representation of three breakpoints applied to a page. In this example, the first breakpoint might represent a large tablet, the second could be a small tablet, and the third a mobile device.

---

[4] Ethan Marcotte, *Responsive Web Design* (A Book Apart, 2011).

Suppose you have a 600-square-foot room that starts to shrink. At about 550 square feet, things start rubbing against each other and the room is cramped, so you resize the furniture and adjust the room's layout. The room then continues to shrink, and when it hits 500 square feet, you again have to adapt the room's layout. In this metaphor, your room's breakpoints are at 600 square feet, 550 square feet, and 500 square feet, because these are the points at which your layout starts to break.

Some designers like using standardized breakpoints, built specifically for mobile, tablet, and desktop variations. I prefer starting with a mobile-first website and then growing the site from there. In my method, I expand the site gradually, and once the layout starts to look off or has excessive space at the sides, I insert a breakpoint and start to adjust as gradually as possible.

1.2   *Building your first responsive site*

Now that you have an understanding of what the responsive web is, it's time to dive into building a responsive site. In the rest of this chapter, we'll walk through the fundamentals of a responsive site build. For this chapter, it's important that you have some basic understanding of HTML and CSS. If you're an absolute beginner, pick up Rob Crowther's *Hello! HTML5 & CSS3* (Manning, 2012) or find another introductory resource to get started. I'll try to break the concepts down a bit, but it might be helpful to do some research if you find yourself getting lost.

First we'll create a prototype. When building a responsive site, I normally use rapid prototyping, because I can quickly view and arrange content in the browser. Rapid prototypes are written in HTML, so they render in mobile and tablet browsers as well as desktop browsers. This gives teams a distinct advantage once the actual design phase approaches.

Then we'll discuss how to interpret a traditional layout, like one you might get from an art director in the form of a Photoshop, Fireworks, InDesign, or Illustrator file. We'll discuss how to take the components of a full site design and interpret them to create the markup for a mobile site. After that, we'll cover how to use percentages to build the site layout, and I'll show you how to implement responsive images. Then we'll get hands-on with our first breakpoint.

This is some exciting stuff, and this chapter will build some of the foundations that will carry you through the rest of the book. This is by no means all there is to the responsive web, but it's at least the tip of the iceberg.

1.2.1   *Creating prototypes*

When I was a teenager, I loved to work with my hands. I'd build toolbox after toolbox in my high school shop class. I'd build one and think to myself, "This is good, but it's not great," and immediately want to do it again. Every night I'd snip, bend, and weld these little metal boxes, and each toolbox I made was better than the last, improving my technique and adding little tweaks here and there.

Creating prototype after prototype made it so that when I took my final exam, I knew exactly how the toolbox should be built. The same is true for responsive sites. By prototyping before you build, you make sure that you're creating a site that communicates your vision clearly. For both the designer and developer, rapid prototyping is essential. Rapid prototyping is the process of building a site for exploratory purposes. There are a few different approaches to rapid prototyping, and we'll use Foundation 3, by Zurb.

Foundation is a front-end framework for rapid site production. It offers a suite of tools for making front-end development simple, but like all frameworks it requires strict adherence to its own system. As a result, I use it only for quickly building prototypes. I still prefer starting from scratch when I produce a site, but getting ideas into a browser early on is fantastic.

Developer insight: Foundation versions

I wrote this chapter using Foundation 3, and the Foundation library has since been updated. At the time of this writing, Foundation 5 is the latest version.

The list of features available in Foundation is fairly exhaustive. Included in the basic framework are

- A responsive grid system
- Navigation elements, including sliders and tabs
- Buttons and forms
- jQuery plug-ins for modal pop-ups and tooltips, as seen in figure 1.6

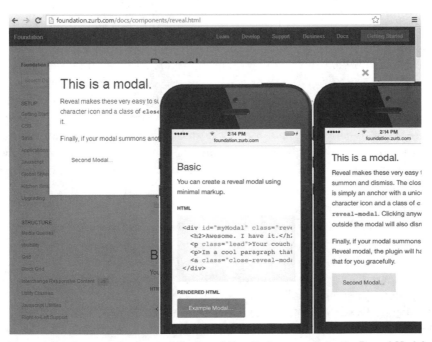

Figure 1.6   An example of one of the Foundation Zurb components, the Reveal Modal

Most prototyping frameworks are relatively similar, and though I discourage using prototype markup in a production-ready site build, Foundation is relatively clean for production if necessary. Foundation is available as a free download from http://foundation.zurb.com.

Developer insight: rapid prototyping

Rapid prototyping is your first line of defense in the war against bad ideas. Because the responsive web is constantly in flux and every element on the page needs to be agile enough to refactor itself, getting in ahead of design and identifying modules and page templates is the best way to guide a conversation. When prototyping, it's common to find out that there are easier ways for users to accomplish goals, or that an element is completely unnecessary.

The most important plus of rapid prototyping, though, is that it gives you an incomplete but usable piece of the site that you can discuss with your team and can interact with across devices. Remember, until something is actually created, it's purely speculative. I'm regularly asked to attend meetings or review creative work from designers to try and find out whether or not ideas will work. I make my best guess, but I can never truly know unless I have time to build a prototype and experiment. In my experience, that's where some of the most innovative work comes from—the sense of exploration that comes with building a prototype.

FROM SKETCH TO PROTOTYPE

We'll prototype a redesign for a developer blog. We'll use a blog as our example because it's one of the few kinds of sites every developer has experience with. Everyone who builds websites starts with their own blog or portfolio site. Even if you've never built a website, you've probably considered what your site would need to have on it.

Because we want to keep the site extremely simple, we'll work from a rough sketch. Generally *sketches*, like the one shown in figure 1.7, are transformed into *wireframes*, which serve as an early articulation of a website's layout and functionality.

As you can see, this rough draft gives you a model for building your prototype. You can clearly tell what elements are on the page and get a general sense of their relationships. It's just enough to get you started.

USING MARKUP TO CREATE A PROTOTYPE

Most of the CSS and JavaScript you'll need to use in Foundation is already there for you. It's just a matter of writing your markup to fit it, and luckily the markup is straightforward. For a full reference to the Foundation 3 source code, check out the book's chapter 1 source code directory. The 1.1 folder contains a starter template for this Foundation prototype.

We'll start by writing the HTML code for the header area. You need to set the header aside as the first row, and then work inside that row to separate areas based on

We'll use placeholder images to get a sense of image size and relationship. We don't want to spend a lot of time working through the creative aspects of these images just yet.

These buttons will be generated using preset elements in the Foundation framework.

Some scratch notes on the side can be useful reminders, if you can manage to read them.

We'll use placeholder text to give us a sense of the copy.

Foundation has a handy framework for forms, which we'll be taking advantage of for this mini contact form.

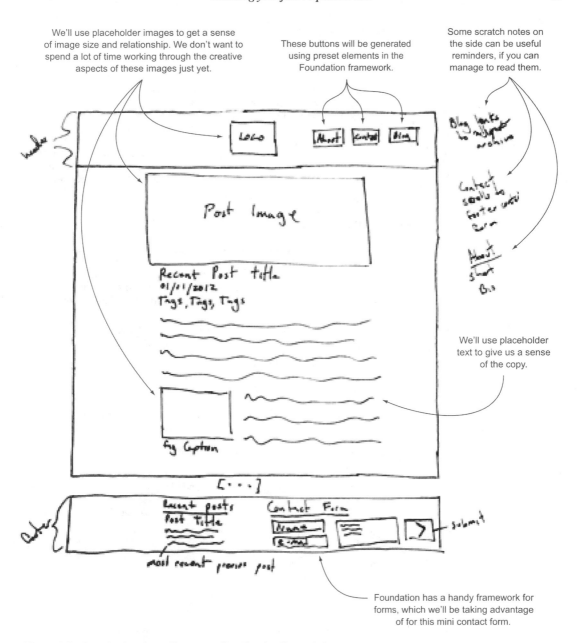

Figure 1.7   **Rough sketches offer some direction for the prototype.**

Foundation's built-in 12-column grid system. The source code for this is in the 1.2 folder:

Declare a row to start the section off.

By stating "two columns" you can apply the desired spacing for your elements and add offsets (blank spacing) using the "offset" classes.

Serving placeholder images from placehold.it is a simple way of showing where images belong and roughly what size they should be.

Here you need to add a little whitespace, so offset the column by two column widths.

```
<div class="row">
<div class="two columns offset-by-five">
    <img src="http://placehold.it/300x200" />
</div>
<div class="three columns offset-by-two">
  <a class="small button">About</a>
  <a class="small button">Blog</a>
  <a class="small button">Contact</a>
</div>
</div>
```

The button class gives you buttons to imply interface elements. These buttons can be accompanied by adjectives to describe their size (tiny, small, medium, large), as well as their relationship to the rest of the interface (such as success, alert, or secondary buttons).

With this little snippet of code, you've produced a simple header for the prototype. Now that you have a header, you can add a footer before moving on to adding the content. The full source code is in the 1.2 folder:

```
<div class="row">
  <div class="three columns">
    <h5>Previous Post</h5>
    <h6>Post Title</h6>
    <p>Lorem ipsum dolor sit amet, consectetur adipisicing elit, sed do
    eiusmod</p>
    <a href="#">Read More</a>
  </div>
  <div class="seven columns">
    <div class="row">
      <div class="nine columns">
        <h5>Contact</h5>
        <input type="text" placeholder="Name" />
        <input type="text" placeholder="E-mail" />
        <textarea placeholder="Message"></textarea>
      </div>
      <div class="three columns">
        <h5> </h5>
        <input type="button" value="Submit" class="large button" />
      </div>
    </div>
  </div>
</div>
```

Foundation has styles in place for form elements. These are extremely helpful in discovering usability issues.

This blank <h5> is just for spacing purposes. Because the prototype is just for internal use, you don't need to worry too much about making your markup pretty.

In just a few lines of code, you've been able to produce a browser-based prototype that can be hosted in a development environment and shared with the rest of the team. For designers, this can be a powerful tool in anticipating the layout of a site, and for developers, a model in the browser allows them to conceptualize the responsive elements of a site.

If you scale your browser window down, you'll see how the site starts to break down in smaller screens. If you immediately jump into the mobile view, you'll see that your header breaks down and gets a little clunky. Fortunately, the Foundation framework offers you control over what your prototype looks like as your viewport changes.

USING RAPID PROTOTYPES TO CREATE CONTENT

One of the advantages of using a rapid prototype is the ability to quickly view and arrange content in the browser. For instance, if you're doing a redesign of a blog site, you can post existing blog articles, images, and videos into the prototype and view how the content interacts. Through this sort of exploration, you can discover facets of the site that might remain undiscovered until later in the project.

Before you use a rapid prototype, you need to define what type of content you want to arrange. Defining content types is important in the responsive web for two reasons:

- Defining content early can identify why the user is visiting the site, and you can prioritize according to user needs.
- Once you identify the content types in a site, you can start building a content well. A *content well* is a collection of assets, such as images, articles, and copy for the site.

Looking at the sketch, you can see that there are two different content types, a large image and an article, with a headline, tags, and a date. We're going to want to replicate these in the prototype. The full source code can be found in the 1.3 folder:

```
<article class="row">
  <header class="twelve columns">
    <figure>
      <img src="http://placehold.it/980x400?text=Post+Image" />
    </figure>
    <h1>Recent Post Title</h1>
  </header>
  <div class="twelve columns">
    <aside class="three columns">
      <div class="row">
        <div class="eleven columns panel">
          <h5>01/01/2012</h5>
          <p><span class="label">Tag</span> [...]</p>
        </div>
      </div>
    </aside>
    <p>Lorem ...</p>
    <p>Lorem ...</p>
    <p>Lorem ...</p>
    <p>Lorem ...</p>
  </div>
</article>
```

You can nest rows within rows. This way you have a little more control over the sizing and spacing of elements. A nested row is still composed of twelve columns.

Twelve columns will fill the row and will also ensure consistent padding throughout the rest of the page. Every column has a padding of 15 px applied to the left and right.

Here's an example of the label class.

The panel class is used to give the element a little grey background. It's useful in distinguishing certain elements on the page.

Figure 1.8   With just a little markup, you're well on your way to a functional prototype.

The preceding markup produces a rather respectable prototype (figure 1.8).

You'll notice that this prototype deviates slightly from the sketch earlier in figure 1.7. Once I got the content into place, I noticed that the date and tags looked better floated to the left. I also made the content appear a little bulkier by expanding it from end to end on the page. This is an example of the kind of insight you can gain by building a prototype.

With a built prototype, you can assert some of the basic structure of your site. Although the prototype itself can be used as a fully formed responsive site, I recommend ditching it once you move on to building the actual site. Although a framework like Foundation is great for building quick prototypes, responsive websites should be built with custom CSS, so that each site is as efficient as possible.

With this in mind, we'll move on to building a basic responsive layout. We'll start from scratch to focus on the needs presented by a very simple design and demonstrate some basic CSS concepts used in responsive web design. We'll return to the preceding prototype later in the book.

1.3   *The basic responsive layout*

In the responsive web, designers and developers strive to circumvent the need to design multiple layouts for various screen sizes. Comprehensive layouts (comps), which worked well for print publications and early websites, are too limiting for responsive design. This is where developers come in. Developers can translate the design into the language of the internet using HTML, CSS, and JavaScript for front-end development. Earlier we talked about using rapid prototypes to help bridge the gap between a responsive front end and the design, but for now let's focus on how to take that full-screen layout and turn it into a responsive website.

COMPREHENSIVE LAYOUTS (COMPS)   In advertising, a comprehensive layout (or *comp* for short) is a static image used to represent the final composition of a site. It's an element left over from the days of print advertising, and it served its purpose well back then. Comps were also handy in the early days of web design because of the lack of variation in screen sizes. Unfortunately, comps are too limiting for responsive design because they don't speak to the scalability of a site.

You can look at a website's composition and make some basic assumptions about what can stay, what can be refactored, and what needs to go to save space in a small-screen (mobile) environment. Let's look at our example layout (figure 1.9) and make a few of these assumptions about how we can build this mobile-first.

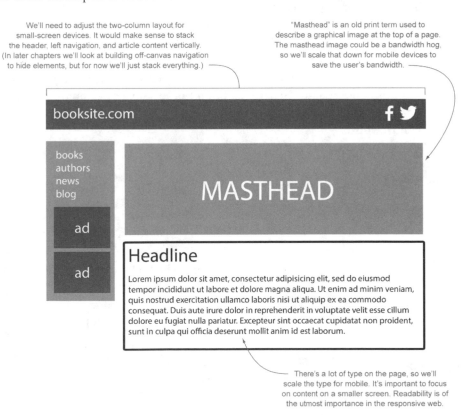

Figure 1.9   Inspecting the design can reveal something about the site's intent.

With a few assumptions in place, we now have a plan for converting this full-screen website design into a mobile-first site.

Developer insight: the CSS box model

I find it's important to keep the basic CSS box model in mind when making layout assumptions. The page will flow, by default, from top to bottom, and then from left to right (or right to left, depending on your use of CSS floats). You can easily float objects left or right once you expand the layout, but with your markup, make sure to put the first (and most important) elements at the top of the document, and then work down the page.

1.3.1   *Mobile-first markup*

First we'll address the markup of the page. This way we can focus on writing HTML in the most efficient manner possible. We'll deal with the CSS a little later in the chapter, but because writing efficient code is so important to the responsive web, I want to spend a little time explaining practices that will make your markup as clean and semantically correct as possible. This will also be beneficial later, as you expand your site into tablet and desktop versions. You'll need to go over the same code multiple times, so take your time and write good, clean code.

Our goal in writing the markup is simple: convert the content into HTML. We'll use some basic placement elements, but ideally we want to keep things as lean as possible. This is good practice in general, but it's especially important in responsive development. CSS and JavaScript are flexible, but your markup should stay consistent between viewports.

Let's start with some standard stuff. Because we'll go through basic site structure and CSS, I'll throw in a doctype declaration and html, head, and body tags. This code can be found in the 1.4 folder in the sample code:

Declare the doctype. This lets the browser know the page is written in HTML5.

```
<!doctype html>
<html>
<head>

<link rel="stylesheet" href="screen.css">

</head>
<body>

</body>
</html>
```

This is the html tag. It's the base tag in any website.

The head tag is where you enclose all of the information the browser needs to render the page properly.

This is the link to the stylesheet, which is written in CSS.

This is the body tag, which is where all of the displayed page content goes.

From here you can start interpreting the markup to create a responsive site. The first thing you want is a `container` div. This will prevent the site from being too fluid and becoming unstable between breakpoints.

Note that in the following code the closing tag is followed by a comment identifying the div's selector. This will remind you what the closure applies to. Because responsive design is highly iterative, these comments can be life savers:

```
<!doctype html>
<html>
<head>

<link rel="stylesheet" href="screen.css">

</head>
<body>
<div class="container">
</div>
<!-- end .container -->
</body>
</html>
```

Using a container to wrap the page can be very helpful in scaling the site. In more complex designs, you'll want to use multiple containers sharing the same class.

As the page grows, it'll be incredibly helpful to have these comments to show you where your elements close. Just remember to remove the comments from production code.

Next, we'll start creating page elements. We'll model the DOM on a left-to-right, top-to-bottom structure. This will provide a logical flow when we're expanding into the wider view. This code can be found in the 1.5 directory in the sample code.

Let's start with the main layout structure:

```
<div class="container">
    <header class="main">

    </header>
    <!-- end header.main -->
    <aside class="main">

    </aside>
    <!-- end aside.main -->
    <section class="content">
        <header class="masthead">
        </header>
        <!-- end header.masthead -->
        <article>

        </article>
        <!-- end article -->
    </section>
    <!-- end section.content -->
</div>
<!-- end .container -->
```

This header will serve as the site-wide header.

This aside will be the site navigation.

The section with the class of "content" will serve as the main content area. This is where the article copy will end up.

Here's the masthead for the content section. In this block you'll call the article masthead.

This article tag is where you'll directly control the written article for the page.

There are a few things to note in this example. First, I recommend using classes to define the areas you're marking up. This will give you repeatable classes to use throughout the site and more streamlined CSS.

You've established the structure, so now you can start placing content into the page. In general, when writing your initial mockup, it helps to keep in mind that you should write as little as possible.

Let's get into the details of the markup. We'll start with `<header class="main">`:

We'll use CSS to display an image in the site logo, but it's good form to write out the site name, in case the CSS isn't loaded.

```
<header class="main">
  <h1 id="logo">book-site.com</h1>
  <div class="social">
    <a class="icon twitter" href="javascript:void(0);">twitter</a>
    <a class="icon facebook" href="javascript:void(0);">facebook</a>
  </div>
</header>
<!-- end header.main -->
```

For these temporary links, we'll use javascript void, instead of the more common #. This keeps the page from returning to the top when you click the link.

Next, you can start marking up the `aside` block, which will contain secondary elements such as navigation and advertisements:

```
<aside class="main">
  <nav>
    <a href="javascript:void(0);">books</a>
    <a href="javascript:void(0);">authors</a>
    <a href="javascript:void(0);">news</a>
    <a href="javascript:void(0);">blog</a>
  </nav>
  <div class="ads">
    <figure class="ad">
      <img src="images/ad.jpg" />
    </figure>
    <figure class="ad">
      <img src="images/ad.jpg" />
    </figure>
  </div>
  <!-- end .ads -->
</aside>
```

This `<nav>` tag will serve as the primary site navigation.

This is the container for the ads.

The `<figure>` tag serves as a semantic wrapper for responsive images.

Notice that the `<img>` tag on the page is wrapped with a `<figure>` tag. The `<figure>` tag will be used as a responsive image wrapper to scale the image with CSS. It's a handy little trick, and I like to use the wonderfully semantic `<figure>` tag, as opposed to using a `<div>` with an `image-wrap` class. We'll cover responsive images in the next section, when we start talking about CSS.

With a little more HTML code, you'll have all of the markup you need to start styling the page:

```
<section class="main">
<article>
  <header class="masthead">
    <figure>
      <img src="images/masthead.jpg" />
    </figure>
```

Because the masthead is important to the article below, it's included in the article tag.

```
    </header>
    <!-- end header.masthead -->
    <h2>Headline</h2>
    <p>Lorem ipsum dolor sit amet, [...]</p>
</article>
</section>
<!-- end section.main -->
```

The headline follows the masthead.

The ellipsis shortens the placeholder copy for the sake of brevity.

Now you should have something that looks like figure 1.10.

This page will function as your raw material. By throwing all of your content out there, you have a base to start from and you can begin to style the page. It's not uncommon to find that you need to add some helpers to the page, but because you're taking a mobile-first approach here, it's important to strive for as light a page as possible.

1.3.2 Using percentages in CSS

You can now start styling the page. This is where the rubber really meets the road in responsive design.

When you build anything physical in this world, you assign it some values. Say you're building a birdhouse. You can make that birdhouse 6 inches long, 7 inches

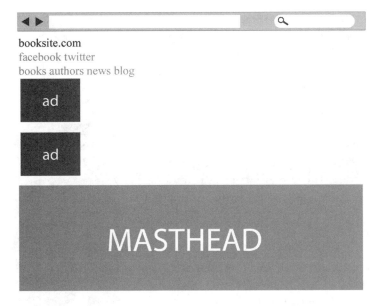

Figure 1.10 The page in raw, unstyled markup

wide, and 5 inches tall. When you're done, you're done. It's a 6 x 7 x 5 birdhouse, for-ever and always. That birdhouse can never adapt to fit bigger birds or shrink to fit in a smaller tree, but on a web page you can do exactly that.

If you could build a flexible birdhouse that's 5% as tall as the tree it's in and then the tree grows, the birdhouse would grow with it, and then bigger birds could live inside it. Percentages give you a fluid model to base your site's structure on. With per-centages, every element becomes relative to its parent element. We'll dive into this subject more in chapter 5.

So how can you turn the previous very static web page blueprint into a magically expanding birdhouse?

USING CONTAINERS

Let's start by defining the context. Because we're adopting a mobile-first approach, we'll start by defining the container element with a little CSS. The CSS for the follow-ing examples can be found in the 1.7 source code folder:

```
.container{
    width:240px;          ⟵——— This width will be expanded later using media queries.
    margin:0 auto;
}
```

With the container defined, you can start putting some other pieces in place. The con-tainer will be the expanding birdhouse; as the content needs to grow, this container will grow to accommodate it.

Now you need to start setting up the contents of this container. You need to ensure that the containers are fluid, so that they can grow and shrink to meet your needs.

WHOLES, HALVES, AND QUARTERS

At its core, the mobile grid is broken into wholes, halves, and quarters. This is a very simple grid, and it works extremely well for small-screen devices (see fig-ure 1.11). By using such a rudimentary grid, you'll find it's easier to understand content areas and how they interact.

Important areas, or areas that serve as wrappers for quarantined content, get to be wholes, occupying 100% of their parent. Other areas can be halves or quarters, depending on their priority and how they interact with the rest of the page.

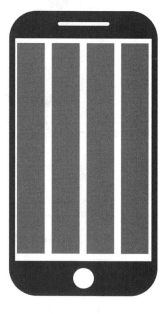

Figure 1.11   A four-column grid for mobile websites

You know that the header, aside, and content sections will fill the entire width of the container by stacking vertically on top of each other, so they can take advantage of all the space allotted to them:

```
*.main{
    width:100%;
    padding:10px 0;
}
```

With the width set to 100%, every element with the main class will occupy all of the width within the parent element.

With the preceding code, all of the main blocks will fill out the width and stack nicely. Now let's add a little styling and jump ahead a bit:

```
header.main{background:#4d4d4d; height:16px;}
aside.main{background:#e4e4e4; height:16px;}
```

These rules assign colors to aside.main and header.main.

```
h1#logo{
    width:50%;
    height:20px;
    float:left;
    background:url(/images/logo.jpg) no-repeat top left;
    text-indent:-99999px;
}

.social{
    width:50%;
    float:left;
}
```

Set a width of 50% so the two elements each occupy 50% of their parent elements—in this case, header.main.

```
.icon{
    width:25px;
    height:20px;
    display:block;
    float:right;
    margin:0 10px 0 0;
    text-indent:-99999px;
}
```

Using the class of icon to give the rules for both of the icons avoids repetition, because they both function similarly.

Using the unique .facebook and .twitter classes, you can specify images for each of the links.

```
.icon.facebook{background:url(/images/facebook.jpg) no-repeat top right;}
.icon.twitter{background:url(/images/twitter.jpg) no-repeat top right;}
```

There's a lot going on in this bit of CSS. First of all, you give two elements, #logo and .social, block percentage–based rules. This ensures they'll always occupy 50% of their parent. If the parent (header.main) occupies 320 px, then div.social and h1#logo will each occupy 160 px. If the header scales up to 640 px, then div.social and h1#logo will each occupy 320 px.

When you know that you have even halves or quarters, percentages can be easy. It gets more complicated when you have to make a percentage-based layout based on fixed creative design. Later in the book, we'll go into depth on how to do that.

You've already set the `<aside class="main">` to 100%. Now let's add the following code to the stylesheet to break the links into quarters of the navigation area. This gives the links a good amount of interactive space:

```
nav{
  width:100%;
}

nav a{
  display:block;
  float:left;
  width:25%;
  text-align:center;
  text-decoration: none;
  color:#333;
}
```

← **This call of 25% will break the four navigation links into quarters, each occupying 25% of the page.**

Now we just need to apply some CSS to clean up the ads:

```
.ads figure{
  width:50%;
  display:block;
  float:left;
  padding-top:10px;
}

.ads figure img{
  display:block;
  margin:0 auto;
}
```

Split the two figure tags, wrapping the ads into halves.

With margin:0 auto;, the images will remain centered in the parent figure tag.

Using some simple, fluid CSS, you've managed to organize the site in an orderly manner and add some logical navigation.

1.3.3   Adding text and images

Now that the primary navigation and site header are in place, you can start dropping in content. Because this is a rudimentary mobile site, the content will follow below the navigation, preserving the hierarchy from the design. We'll include a masthead, a headline, and a few paragraphs of placeholder text.

Earlier you wrote the markup for this; now you just need to add the content. To review, the markup looks like this:

```
<article>
  <header class="masthead">
    <figure>
      <img src="images/masthead.jpg" />
      </figure>
  </header>
  <!-- end header.masthead -->
  <h2>Headline</h2>
  <p>Lorem ipsum dolor sit amet, [...]</p>
</article>
</section>
<!-- end section.main -->
```

Content is king in the responsive web. Every site I've ever visited, I visited because the site contained some information that I wanted. Because of my profession, sometimes that information relates to design choices or code snippets, but in general, people browsing the web are looking for content. In later chapters, I'll focus on this topic in depth.

For now, let's just focus on two important factors:

- Display images fluidly, so they can be easily resized with the browser window.
- Apply scalable CSS to the text, so you can adjust font sizes for various devices.

Before you can do this, you have to set the context of the `<article>` tag. This tag will serve as the wrapper for the text, headline, and images it contains. You can apply some simple CSS to accomplish this wrapping:

```
article{
   width:100%;
}
```

SCALABLE IMAGES

In the article's masthead, there's a large image that will need to be shrunk down. This is how you can scale images for responsive web development:

```
.masthead{
   width:100%;
   padding-bottom:10px;
}

figure{
   width:100%;
}

figure img{
   width:100%;
   max-width:1000px;
   height:auto;
   display:block;
   margin:0 auto;
}
```

Start by setting the `<figure>` tag to have a width of 100%.

Repeat the width of 100%.

The max-width will prevent the image from exceeding its native size. This way you won't lose any image quality caused by the image scaling above its native size.

The height:auto rule will maintain the image's aspect ratio.

Set display:block and margin:0 auto to keep the image centered if it scales beyond the max-width of 1000 px.

We'll use the `<figure>` tag because it's intended as a semantic wrapper for images. This makes more sense than using a div with an `image-wrap` class, because you should always strive to use semantic markup. Some sort of wrapper is necessary in order to properly scale the containing image. The `<img>` will occupy 100% of the `<figure>` wrapper.

Luckily, all browsers can scale images and preserve their aspect ratio—the image's proportional relationship between width and height. An image that's 1000 x 500 pixels can scale down to 100 x 50 pixels for a mobile device and still look great. In fact, for devices with higher pixel density, such as the Apple Retina display, this can create a desirable effect by doubling the image's pixel density.

It should be noted that downloading a large 1000 x 500 pixel image on a small-screen device will require the user to download a lot of data they don't need. There are a few ways of serving responsive images that have been in use for a while, but there still isn't a satisfying solution in the HTML specifications.

By giving the image a `max-width` of 1000 px and centering it inside the figure tag, you ensure that the image doesn't look broken if the figure tag extends beyond 1000 px. This is a safety measure to ensure that the site retains its wonderful layout in a wide-screen monitor.

1.3.4 *The fickle and mighty em*

Now that you have a fluid masthead image, it's time to focus on the text. Adjustable text is another foundational element in the responsive web. People read copy differently depending on the device they're using. For example, a desktop monitor might be further away from a user than a handheld device.

Personally, I like text on all of my devices to be large, because I don't like having the device too close to my face. Because of this, my devices commonly have a higher default text size. This inevitably breaks layouts that aren't designed with fluidity in mind. If a site is built with an ebb and flow for content using less-rigid CSS, my text-size preferences shouldn't affect the layout.

How is this achieved? The answer is in em values. Em values are a little hard to understand, because they're abstract and can change at the drop of a hat. Historically, front-end development has had an emphasis on pixel perfection, and developers have typically used pixel control. Pixels are literal, stiff, and consistent. Twelve-pixel type is exactly 12 pixels (except on a Retina display, which has quadruple the pixel density, so 1 pixel unit is actually 4 pixels). The em, in contrast, is a bit fickle, but once you master it, it's highly rewarding.

The trick to using ems is that the em is a cascading size. Browsers have a default base font size, usually 16 px. This would make 1 em equal to 16 px by default.

Imagine you have an `<h1>` that has a `font-size` of 2 em: that `<h1>` would be 32 px. Now say you need a smaller block of text within that `<h1>`, so you write this:

```
<h1> Headline <small>Sub-Head</small></h1>
```

With CSS, you'd apply this rule:

```
h1{
  font-size:2em;
}

h1 small{
  font-size:0.75em;
}
```

The `<h1>` takes the default font size (16px) and multiplies it by its em size (2em) to get the applied `font-size` (which would appear as 32px). The font size would then cascade to the child tag, which in turn sets the font size to `0.75em`, so the parent `font-size` (which appears as 32px) is multiplied by the child selector (`0.75em`) to get the new size (32 x 0.75 = 24px).

Let's apply this to the web page. First give the `<h1>` its sizing. (Resist the urge to reset the body type to 16 px, as most resets are prone to do, in order to respect the user's browser settings.) Because it's a header, let's make it considerably bigger than the rest of the type:

```
article h1{
  font-size: 1.5em;
}
```

If the user has their default type size set to 16 px, this header will appear to be 24 px.

You can leave the paragraph text set to 1 em, because that's a default setting for paragraphs, but let's suppose that you know you're going to be including some bold text inline that needs to be bigger. You could do this by adding a rule of `font-size: 1.1em` to the `<strong>` tag, written in CSS as follows:

```
p strong{font-size:1.1em;}
```

We'll discuss the details of using ems in depth in chapter 6, where we'll compare using pixels and ems in responsive design, and discuss how to manipulate cascading em sizes to your benefit. For now, just keep in mind that ems should only be applied directly to text elements such as `<span>`, `<p>`, `<h1>` through `<h6>`, `<small>`, and `<big>`.

Avoid setting ems directly on elements on the page—this can cause problems when the font sizes cascade. Suppose you need a particular size text, but only in a given element, in a scenario like this:

```
<div class="promotional-area">
  <span>EXTRA BIG TEXT</span>
</div>
```

Instead of doing this,

```
span{font-size:5em; /* big text */}
```

try doing this:

```
.promotional-area span{font-size:5em; /* big text */}
```

Or use a helper class, like this:

```
<div class="promotional-area">
  <span class="big-text">EXTRA BIG TEXT</span>
</div>
```

```
span.big-text{font-size:5em; /* big text */}
```

You should now have a rough little demo site, but if you expand your browser, you'll see that you only have a mobile site. The entire point of the responsive web is to build sites that are fluid, so this simply won't do. The responsive web is all about adjusting layouts for various devices. Now it's time to apply the core concepts of the responsive web: media queries and breakpoints.

1.3.5   *Your first breakpoint*

As you gain experience building responsive sites, you'll get a feel for where to set breakpoints, but for now we'll set one at 600 px. In this instance, 600 px is kind of arbitrary; a good rule of thumb with responsive sites is that you should insert breakpoints whenever the site breaks. If the layout starts to fall apart, you add a breakpoint and fix it.

We're trying to get this new mobile site to look like the desktop design when it's expanded, so you need to incrementally adapt the site until it looks like the design in figure 1.11:

```
@media only screen and (min-width: 600px){
  .container{
    width:600px;
  }
}
```

Here you declare the rules that must be met before the CSS in the media query takes effect.

All CSS within the brackets of the media query takes precedence over the existing rules

With this simple rule, the container div has taken a new shape.

Now you can begin the work of refactoring your layout to match the design. CSS rules within a media query have a higher specificity. The media query itself has a specificity value that's added to the selector's overall specificity.

Developer insight: CSS specificity

CSS rules are applied using *selectors* and can cascade over one another. Every element on a page has a number of ways of attaching rules, each one with its own value. The value applied to a selector is referred to as its *specificity*.

A class has a small value, an ID has a greater value, and !important declarations have a huge value. Media queries are involved in calculating these values.

If you have some JavaScript experience, you might recognize the media query as being similar to an if statement. Basically, @media is like saying "If you're viewing this," and then you state the conditions that validate the media query. In the preceding example, the conditions are only screen and (min-width: 600px).

The first condition is quite literal. The only screen condition means just that: only on a screen. The second condition, (min-width:600px), is slightly more complicated. This could be translated as "at a minimum width of 600 px." If we put the entire query together, it could be read as "If you're viewing this only on a screen at a minimum width of 600 px."

Using the preceding media query, if the browser size meets or exceeds 600 px, the new rules take effect. There are some other subtleties involved in this and several reasons for doing it this way. You're applying new rules only if the browser exceeds a size, as opposed to applying new rules if a browser is under a size as you might do with @media (max-width:600px);. This is beneficial, assuming that a smaller screen means a smaller device, which means limited capabilities.

There you have it, your first responsive website. Approaching site-building in this way, with a prototype, makes building the site easy. Now you can get into adding details and styles, but this will serve as your base.

1.4 *Summary*

In this chapter, we discussed what the responsive web is and its core concepts. You also learned how to build your own responsive site. This chapter has given you all the information you need to make a basic responsive site.

Collaboration is a huge part of your ability to succeed in responsive web design. This chapter's example site is extremely pared down, but with a designer's eye and a coder's hands, you could make something magical. Prototyping gives designers and developers a shared starting point in the creation of a website. Every phase in a website's life is a prototype for its next version, and every version includes a series of small improvements. By prototyping, you get to the first version quickly and can craft your end product from there, with designers and developers collaborating toward a shared goal.

Up next, we'll create a responsive website mobile-first!

1.5 *Discussion points*

Because this book is all about collaboration, each chapter will end with some discussion points as opposed to simple exercises. These discussion points are meant to open up conversations between designers and developers and provide opportunities for teams to explore new ways of working together and collaborating. Although this book will strive to give you the information and tools to create better sites, a lot of the challenge in crafting incredible work comes in finding a balance between team members.

Here are a few discussion points arising from the topics covered in this chapter:

- How do you think responsive web design is challenging the web community?
- How do you see prototypes affecting your process? Do you think that simple prototypes can be used to inform design?
- What do you think the major challenges are in translating a web design from desktop to mobile or vice versa?

Design for mobile first

There's a term I like to use to describe what happens when a project starts to get out of control: "gilding the lily." It's an idiom that's derived from Shakespeare, and it means to unnecessarily embellish something. A lot of gilding of lilies can go on when you assume everybody visiting your website is on a desktop browser.

When you have a 1,600-pixel-wide canvas, you have a lot of space to fill, so you might add more buttons, animation, widgets, and images. If you were only designing for a desktop, that would be great, but the whole idea behind responsive design is to be able to move from one device to the next fluidly. If, after you designed for the desktop, you needed to make the site mobile, you'd have to start hiding buttons and images and navigation. You'd have to stuff and scale and tuck until your 1,600-pixel canvas was crammed into the frame. If you weren't careful, the user would end up

31

loading all that hidden content on their phone, which would slow the load time. After spending all that time cramming, your user with a 3G connection would hit the Back button because your page wasn't loading—not exactly the best user experience. If you're wondering if there's a better way, I'm here to tell you there is.

In 2009, Luke Wroblewski wrote a blog post and later a book titled *Mobile First*, in which he laid out a philosophy of web design and development that asked people to focus first on a mobile experience.[1] It's true that the canvas you begin with is much smaller, but by developing mobile first, you retain control as the site expands, as opposed to losing control as the site shrinks.

In this chapter, you'll create a responsive website mobile-first. I'll first talk a bit more about mobile first and its pros and cons, plus specific challenges designers face when designing for mobile first. Then you'll create a mobile-first site demonstrating how designers can solve the challenges of designing a responsive site.

> ## Developer insight: responsive web design is a team sport
>
> Although this chapter focuses on the design process, you need to remember that the principles behind the process are important even if you only code. Whether or not you have any interest in design, knowing something about the topics covered here will help you speak to art directors and help give you some ideas that you can share with designers.
>
> As a developer, you might not think of yourself as *creative*, but the entire site experience depends on you. You are a creative problem solver, and you bring a unique form of creativity to everything you touch. Clean and efficient code is of the utmost importance in a responsive site, because without it pages will load slowly and the interaction can feel clunky. Take your time to develop sites mobile-first, but with the following goals in mind: use semantic markup, object-oriented CSS, and efficient JavaScript.

2.1   Why mobile-first design

One of the biggest challenges in responsive web design is building a site that evolves and scales consistently. The responsive approach seems too limiting to a lot of designers because the canvas they begin with is so much smaller. But by working within the limitations that exist, you can take control of those limitations. By starting with a smaller screen and scaling up, you afford yourself new opportunities as the screen size expands, and you can make careful additions, as opposed to having to cut a site to pieces and squeeze modules into smaller and smaller spaces as you move to smaller screens.

---

[1] The "Mobile First" blog post is on Luke Wroblewski's Ideation and Design blog, www.lukew.com/ff/entry.asp?933. The book, *Mobile First*, is published by A Book Apart (2011).

The mobile-first approach provides benefits, but it's not a design solution that fits all scenarios or workflows. Thus, in this section we'll look at the benefits of starting small and also at the challenges. Then we'll get started with our mobile-first site.

Designer insight: the cons of mobile-first design

This book applies mobile-first design in order to teach the concept, but in the interest of balance, it should be noted that there are some cons to this approach. There are definitely some points of contention concerning mobile-first design, but all the arguments I hear arise from the difficultly in understanding how to use the negative space created when you expand from mobile to tablet and desktop screens.

The biggest con to mobile-first design is that it isn't easy. It takes time and experience. Unfortunately, it's hard for me to agree that this is really a "con." Web design is a constantly evolving field, and learning new practices is simply a cost of working on the web. Labeling this as a con can be a way of avoiding learning more about and evolving your craft.

Is mobile-first the only way to design a website? No, certainly not. There are some cases where building a mobile website isn't the best approach at all, such as if you're building a company intranet that only operates on the desktop. Mobile-first design is simply a tool for you to use at your discretion, and it's an important topic when discussing responsive web design. You should use it when it makes sense for your project.

2.1.1 Benefits of mobile-first design

Designing for mobile first can feel like a huge step, and it may be a bit of a departure from your current workflow. When embracing a new way of working, it's important to vet the idea and get a good sense of its rewards. Aside from creating a mobile site, designing mobile first offers a wealth of value: because of the limited space on mobile screens, designing mobile first forces you to focus your design, content, and user experience on what your clients and their customers need.

PRIORITIZES CONTENT

Mobile-first allows you to prioritize content and focus on the most important parts of your site early. A mobile screen only has room for the most important content, so you need to make a decision about what's crucial to your site in the early design phases. By loading the essentials first, you'll be able to add functionality as it's needed.

ALLOWS PROGRESSIVE ENHANCEMENT

It's much easier to fill up new space than to squeeze the same content into a smaller space. A while ago I changed apartments. I was living in a small studio and upgraded to a one bedroom, and in my new apartment I found that I had a lot of open space. After a few trips to the store, I filled the space up pretty well. This move gave me the opportunity to expand on what I already had.

A few years later, I moved from Texas to New York City, and apartments in New York are incredibly small compared to Texas. I quickly ran out of space and ended up having to get rid of a lot of furniture. I had to edit what I owned to fit the new, smaller space.

All in all, the move from a small space to a larger one is hugely preferable to a move from a large space to a small one. By designing for mobile first, you can work in the added space as the site expands, instead of trying to cram the existing content into an ever-tightening space.

There are two terms that describe this pattern. One is *progressive enhancement*, and it's the process of starting with a simple base and enhancing it into a more complex product. *Graceful degradation* is the opposite, taking a complex site and building in fallbacks for components that fail. Moving from a mobile environment to larger screens gives you the chance to progressively enhance, whereas reducing a large-screen site to a mobile one is more like graceful degradation. We'll cover this subject in detail in chapter 8.

2.1.2 *The challenges of designing for mobile first*

When designing for mobile first, you'll be presented with some new challenges, such as working on a smaller canvas. Web design is a constantly evolving process, so a constantly changing canvas is nothing new, but designing for both mobile first and the desktop on the same canvas can be a bit of a learning curve.

DECLUTTERING THE SCREEN

With desktop sites, it's easy to let the content get lost in a sea of secondary information. On some sites, content gets shoved to the side to make room for ads, links to other articles and related products, social media integration, or any number of sidebar distractions.

Mobile is a medium of singular focus, as is evident in some of the most popular apps in mobile platforms, such as Twitter or Instagram. The applications put the content front and center and integrate secondary content at intuitive points along the linear content path.

In designing mobile first, you have an excuse to strip away these secondary, confusing elements and focus directly on the content. Take advantage of it. Mobile first may as well be synonymous with "content first," and at its core, a mobile website strategy is a content strategy. Mobile web design is 90% content design and 10% decorative design, as a result of the size, power, and bandwidth limitations.

LIMITING THE INPUT

Another major challenge in mobile-first design is the input limitations. In traditional mouse-and-keyboard computer usage, the input devices are very precise tools. Touch screens only have one input type, a finger. When the first iPhone came out, one of the early complaints was its lack of a physical keyboard. A software-based keyboard can be prone to latency issues, and for people with larger hands, such a keyboard can lead to a lot of errors while typing. These issues have largely been forgotten because the software keyboard on the device screen offered more benefits than problems.

The lack of a mouse adds a new complication to the mix, though: the finger lacks the precision of a mouse. A mouse offers pinpoint accuracy on a clickable object, so interacting with a small button on a page isn't difficult. In contrast, a finger can obscure the object that the user is attempting to click. As a result, all critical elements need to be larger on a mobile screen. That means you have the challenge of less screen space and also the need for bigger elements. We'll explore a few ways you can overcome these issues in this chapter.

Developer insight: coarse or precise pointers

In a current draft of upcoming additions to the CSS specifications, there's a level-four media query for coarse or precise pointers. This would function much like some current media queries but would offer unique styling for pointer types. The media query would classify pointers with limited accuracy, such as touch screens, as *coarse*, and devices with accurate pointing, such as a mouse, as *precise*.

These media queries would be called as follows:

```
@media (pointer:coarse){}
```

Currently this hasn't been adopted, but with some luck it might be. For now, developers can identify touch devices singularly by using Modernizr. For more information on how to do this, see chapter 8, which focuses on Modernizr and progressive enhancement.

The thing that initially holds many designers back from mobile-first web design is that they're being hit with a smaller screen and fewer resources. But with a bit of practice, working within these limitations quickly becomes second nature.

In the next section, we'll take the prototype and wireframes we built in chapter 1 and start designing mobile first. Because site-level headers are the primary interface for our site, we'll start there.

It's all in the name: high-fidelity wireframes

When you're presenting wireframes to a client, you might think introducing a prototype could be confusing. One easy way to contextualize prototypes is by referring to them as "high-fidelity wireframes." This can be reassuring and communicates that a rapid prototype is still a rough sketch, even though it's written in code and is viewable in the browser. Because of its interactive nature, high-fidelity wireframes are a higher-value deliverable as well.

2.2   Designing headers for small screens

The header in the prototype (figure 1.7) includes navigation links to the right (about, contact, and blog). We'll also add some additional content to the left as an information drawer to give the user some more context for the site. To display these elements on a smaller screen in a way that provides an optimal user experience, we'll look at the off-canvas design pattern.

Design patterns are reusable solutions for addressing recurring problems. With off-canvas navigation, we can solve the problem of optimizing the user experience (making the screen less cluttered) by hiding the elements to the left or right side of the page, and when cued, the navigation slides out. This is the pattern used by Facebook and Path for hiding the main navigation and allowing the user to focus on the immediately important information.

Let's get started designing these headers for the small screen.

2.2.1   Creating the header

We'll start by designing the header's unaltered state. We'll give it two buttons that we can later use to cue the off-canvas navigation (see figure 2.1).

We have two simple icons in the header, both about 44 x 44 pixels (the minimum target size recommended by Apple for the original iPhone Human Interface Guidelines), and a logo to reinforce that the visitor is in the right place. On the left is an information icon. To the right is a three-bar navigation icon—this is becoming a standard icon for expanded navigation. We'll use these two buttons to give users a way to navigate deeper into the site.

Because we're using off-canvas navigation, we'll need to show what that navigation looks like, so let's get a sense of the spacing, color, and design of the expanded navigation (see figure 2.2).

Now we have some obvious site navigation. For this site, there are only a few sections to access, but in a large site you could scroll down to see more options. You could also potentially slide the header off further to the left and leave more room for the navigation on the right.

Figure 2.1   An initial design for the header. Notice the two icons in the corners: to the left is one denoting information, and to the right is one denoting site navigation.

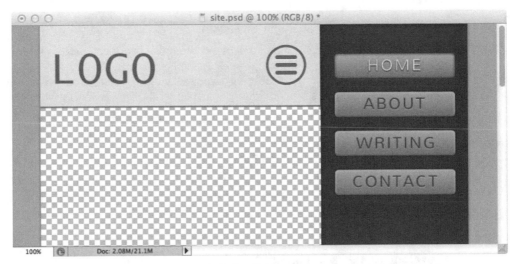

Figure 2.2 The navigation will be expanded when the three-bar navigation icon is pressed.

We can easily apply the same style to the information content on the left side of the page to display some more information about the site's author, content, and so on (see figure 2.3).

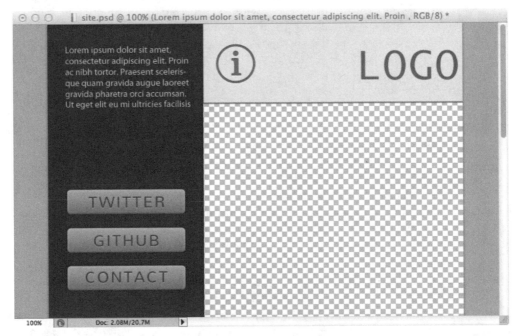

Figure 2.3 On the left side, we provide more information. We also repeat a few links from the right navigation element, which is fine because these links will further inform the user about the subject of the site.

> **Developer insight: off-canvas navigation**
>
> Off-canvas navigation can be a complicated challenge for developers, and there are a few different ways to approach it. One is by simply applying various states as classes on the body element (such as `left-nav-exposed` or `right-nav-exposed`) and adding and removing these classes with jQuery. This is a relatively simple way of accomplishing this task; we'll cover some fancier ways to approach it later.

2.3 *Designing for a touch interface*

As I mentioned earlier, a 44 x 44 pixel size should be the minimum for any clickable target. The user will be engaging the site with a thumb or forefinger, so the target needs to be large enough to easily tap.

> **Developer insight: tap as a hover**
>
> For years, hovering the mouse pointer over an element has been a way of interacting with a page. Users could hover over a page element with their mouse to reveal supplemental content, such as navigation elements or secondary information. In theory, a tap on a touch screen would register as a click, rendering a hover state unusable and the supplemental content hidden.
>
> Fortunately, most mobile browsers have resolved this issue by requiring a second tap on links or elements with a hover state. This double-tapping on mobile browsers is an effective way of ensuring that users can navigate websites, but it's important when developing responsive sites to keep this feature in mind.

In mobile-first body content design, you'll want to ensure that you provide control interactions that don't interfere with the main content of the site. You should use font families and sizes that are easily legible on a digital screen and avoid crowding the screen with links. Large text in a mobile environment is great because it ensures that the user can comfortably read the page without having to hold the phone too close to their face.

It's also a good idea to use simple background patterns, as opposed to large images, which will slow page loading. Although it's easy to believe that users want the same things on small-screen devices as they do on desktops, it's important not to ignore the context implied by a smaller viewport.

> **Developer insight: patterns and Base64 encoding**
>
> In chapter 9 we'll look at methods of improving site performance, and one of those ways is to use Base64 encoding on images. When implementing small, subtle image patterns, try using Base64 image encoding directly in the CSS to avoid having to make

(continued)
an additional server request for more assets. Adding the image data directly to the CSS will increase the total page size somewhat (each image will be about 37% larger when Base64 encoded), but it will improve site load time slightly because the separate requests for each image are eliminated.

2.3.1   *The simplified small-screen grid*

For smaller screens, you need a simplified grid. In chapter 1, I mentioned breaking sites into small grids. I prefer to break them into halves or quarters. Historically, grids have included up to 12 columns, which works in a desktop environment where you have a big width to cover, but on narrow mobile screens, using more than four columns starts to get unmanageable and is too tight for screens smaller than 320 pixels wide. As shown in figure 2.4, four columns give the page a sufficient amount of structure without cluttering the page.

When working in a grid, it's important to keep in mind how the site elements will scale and float. It's best to think of the responsive grid as going from left to right, and then top to bottom. This helps to create a clear and consistent flow of information.

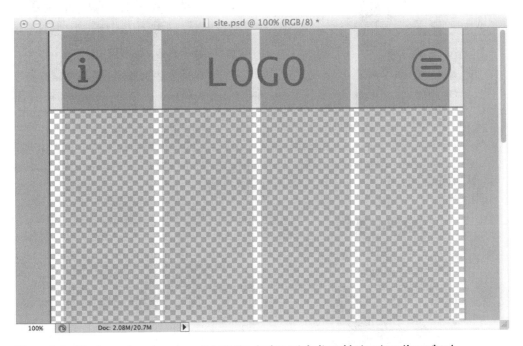

Figure 2.4   The four-column overlay will help the design retain its grid structure throughout the design file.

On a small screen, you might have a one-column grid with four blocks stacked on top of each other, as in figure 2.5. This vertical stacking encourages the user to scroll and keeps the page uncluttered.

As more screen real estate becomes available, the elements can adjust their placement and separate into two columns, as in figure 2.6. The available content area will increase relative to the device screen size.

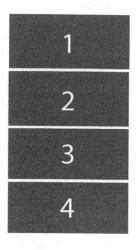

Figure 2.5   Four elements stacked on a small screen

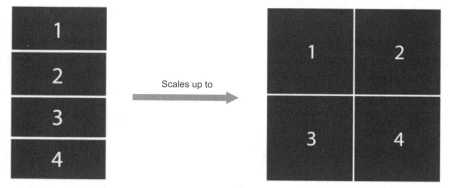

Figure 2.6   The vertically stacked elements can transform into two columns in a mid-sized screen.

This can be extrapolated further as the viewport gets wider and the elements have more horizontal room to fill. This new grid scales up nicely to four columns with four blocks, as shown in figure 2.7.

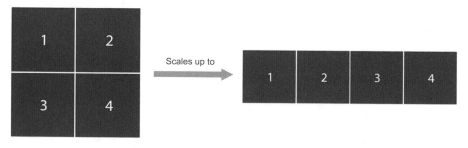

Figure 2.7   The same grid again, now for larger screens

As a designer, you should always anticipate the grid flowing from top to bottom and left to right. This logic can apply to all elements on the page, and grids can even be nested inside grid blocks. It's important to understand and acknowledge this early in the design phase, so you can create sites that take advantage of the way CSS works. This is another reason why prototypes are crucial to responsive design, and why designing in the browser is ultimately the best way to go.

2.4 Designing content for a small screen

Now that you have the grid and navigation, it's time to give the site its content. You first want to ensure that the background will contrast with the body copy. The content of the page is the reason the user is viewing the site, so you want to give it priority and make the site as easy to read as possible.

In figure 2.8, I used a full-width image to enhance the article and set the tone. The full width will be easy to manipulate later, but it also just looks nice.

Figure 2.8   The designed mobile site

You can also see how the design will work with the off-canvas navigation deployed. You want to make sure you don't design these elements in a silo, because you need everything to play nicely together and create an appropriate atmosphere for the user.

Designing for content is tough, and it's one of the biggest reasons that I advocate for the use of prototypes. By prototyping, you can gather content and build a site that meets your client's needs, instead of forcing the client's needs to fit your design.

2.4.1   Using web fonts in layouts

In small-screen design, much of the screen real estate is occupied by type, so one of the best ways to give a site a unique look and feel is with web fonts. Using CSS, you can import web fonts into a stylesheet and use them in your document. The fonts are hosted on the site's server, just like an HTML file or an image, and are loaded into the document. Web fonts can also bog down the page load time for the user, but for the developer it's an efficient and simple way to add a lot of characters to a site. This section will compare the major web font vendors. In chapter 6 you'll learn how to embed the web fonts in a CSS stylesheet.

Historically, designers were limited to using fonts that they could assume visitors had installed on their computers. This meant there were only a handful of typefaces that a designer could confidently design around. Any custom font required in a site design had to be implemented with image replacement, which was a huge burden and made editing and updating sites troublesome and time-consuming for both designers and developers.

The use of fonts online is more limiting than in print, because you need fonts that are licensed for use online, or the site's owners can be fined. But there are several services available to designers to help them use fonts online, most notably Typekit, fonts.com, and Google Fonts.

TYPEKIT

Typekit (https://typekit.com/fonts) was one of the first major font-hosting services available. They were recently bought by Adobe, and their library has expanded dramatically as a result.

Typekit offers a great library and offers reliable cross-browser consistency and the ability to host custom fonts. The downside is that you can't use the fonts locally, and there's a small cost.

Advantages	Disadvantages
High quality and highly optimized fonts	Lacks some of the most popular fonts
Fast to render on the page	
Affordable plans	

FONTS.COM

Fonts.com (www.fonts.com) offers a service similar to Typekit, and it has exclusive rights to several popular font families.

The biggest advantage of fonts.com is that it allows you to download fonts for use in comps, which is nice if you absolutely have to rely on comps. You can also host your own fonts with a fonts.com subscription, a feature that's unavailable through Typekit. Fonts.com also offers the ability to self-host typefaces with certain packages. There's also a cost for using fonts.com.

Advantages	Disadvantages
Has exclusive rights to some very popular font families	Lacks the speed and reliability of Typekit
Fonts available to download for use in comps	
Self-hosting available	

GOOGLE FONTS

Google also hosts a font service, which is free to use and allows you to download the fonts for use locally (www.google.com/fonts). Unfortunately, the selection through Google is limited, and the quality of the fonts isn't as high as on the subscription sites.

Advantages	Disadvantages
Free	Limited selection of fonts
All fonts available for download	Fonts generally of a lower quality

SELF-HOSTING

In addition to web font services, there's also the option of self-hosting fonts on your own server. This gives you the flexibility to use the exact font you want (such as a corporate font for a company site), whereas with a service you're limited to the fonts they have available. This works well if you can acquire and maintain the rights to a font, but purchasing the rights to a web font can be very expensive and it requires a secured hosting environment.

Once you have a client on board to cover the cost, there are a few tricks involved in self-hosting fonts. You first need to be sure you have the bandwidth to serve the typefaces. Second, the type files themselves need to be optimized for web use as well. This means the type needs to be converted into three different formats (WOFF, TrueType, and EOT) in order to cover the formats preferred by the major browsers. (Web fonts are typically available in all three formats, so conversion is only really a concern when the typeface is completely original or extremely rare.) Conversion can compromise the quality of the fonts, but if a custom font is being used, this is an unavoidable consequence. There are processes to improve the quality of web fonts, but they're painstaking and expensive.

Ultimately, self-hosting is a much more difficult technical hurdle than you might expect and can cause some design issues.

Advantages	Disadvantages
High level of control	Often fonts not optimized for web performance, creating issues with aliasing and artifacting
Not limited to available libraries	Can include a very expensive one-time or recurring fee

2.5   Summary

In this chapter, we discussed the beginning phases of designing a site mobile-first. The role of the designer can be the most difficult on a project, because as a designer you have to communicate a brand via an artistic medium that you might not have a high degree of control over. This is the main reason why a designer with little or no experience in CSS is at a huge disadvantage. Web design will always feel like a limiting and confining medium if you don't take the time to learn the details, and ultimately that means designing with CSS.

There's still much to learn about designing responsive web sites. This chapter provides a foundation for some often-unconsidered factors of responsive web design, such as how floats affect objects on the page and web fonts.

Now that you've created a small-screen site, it's time to learn about a new design deliverable that will help you make the transition from PSD (Photoshop Document) to websites. Remember, the goal of responsive design is to not create comps for every single view and every single page. To avoid doing this, in the next chapter you'll learn how to create and communicate design using a style guide.

2.6   Discussion points

- Do you think designing mobile first will help your team be more creative or less?
- Is there anything unique to designing and developing on mobile that's particularly exciting to you?
- How do you think designing for mobile is different from designing for desktop? And if both approaches meet somewhere, where is that?

Part 2

Designing for the responsive web

In this part of the book, we'll start discussing what it takes to design a responsive website. We'll cover what goes into responsive web design from the visual designer's and user-experience (UX) designer's perspectives, but don't think this information won't apply to developers. There's important stuff in here for everyone, and as this book teaches, web design requires collaboration.

In chapter 3 we'll start the discussion with style tiles. These are a new deliverable that makes creating beautiful designs possible, while not dictating layout. By learning to use style tiles, you'll learn how to communicate your design ideas to the client and the development team in an easy-to-understand way.

In chapter 4 we'll begin working on design patterns for building the user experience of a site. I'll show you some example design patterns and offer some explanation about how to start thinking in design patterns.

In chapter 5 we'll cover responsive layouts and discuss some of the challenges and opportunities involved in building them. We'll also discuss content modules and typography in responsive environments.

In chapter 6 we'll dive into how responsive web design affects your site's content. You'll learn how to craft content for mobile, tablet, and desktop screens.

Using style tiles to communicate design

This chapter covers

- What a style guide is and why it's important
- The importance of meaningful client deliverables
- Introduction to style tiles
- Building a style tile

Interior designers use swatches and fabric samples to create a palette to work from. This is an important part of the process; painting and furnishing a room is costly in materials and labor, so setting the color and style ahead of time can help to minimize those expenses.

Style guides function in much the same way, enabling clients to decide on a palette and theme before the hard work of drafting the front end of a website begins. This is important in responsive design, because the website requires a lot of moving parts. Every design element needs to be scalable, flexible, and natively built in CSS in order to maintain a small load burden and efficient architecture.

In order to bridge the gap between mobile, tablet, and desktop sites, you need to visualize the design of a site without implying dimensions, size, or format. Style guides give you the ability to abstract your design and break it into manageable chunks.

In this chapter, you'll learn how to articulate the parts most important to a design and see how to establish a creative visual style for a website without forming the entire site in a graphics editing program. This will let you take a collaborative approach to the actual implementation and create a more vivid and lively website. By breaking away from traditional ways of creating a visual language for a site's design, you open the process up to the fluidity required in responsive design.

Developer insight: understanding design

This chapter is very much focused on the designer. There are no code samples, and we won't really talk about CSS. The entire chapter focuses on design, so why should you care? Why not just skip this chapter entirely? Why include it in this book?

With responsive web design, developers no longer have the luxury of remaining in a silo. The process of design is not something developers can ignore any more. This chapter is part of the book because it's an important part of designing a responsive website. If you're responsible for building the front end of a website, you're responsible for collaborating with the designer, and part of that collaboration is helping advocate for things that will make the process easier. Communicating design is an important technique in the process of website creation.

In a site build I recently was working on, we had a module in the site that wasn't working. It was intended to emulate some 3D motion, but in a 2D plane. The details aren't important—what's important is that the design just wasn't going to work. The designer and I were able to sit down and create something completely new that would work, but this was only possible because I understood his concerns and he understood mine. That understanding facilitated our collaboration.

If you feel like this chapter doesn't concern you, feel free to skip it, but taking an interest in design will make you a better front-end developer.

3.1   *Visualizing design with style guides*

When visualizing a design in traditional web development, working with comprehensive layouts (comps) was the norm. As discussed in chapter 1, comps are static images used to represent a single state of the final coded site. The term *comp*, much like the deliverable itself, is a leftover from the days of print advertising.

The problem with designing in fully laid-out comps is that it assumes too much and fails to communicate the scalability required in responsive web design. Comps are rigid and only represent a single state in a site's design. They're also costly to produce and adjust in responsive design. Finally, they present a false sense of security in the site design's effectiveness. They portray to the client a sort of best-case scenario that rarely reflects the actual use of the site. In a comp, all the content is controlled, but when a site is published and the user or client begins inserting their own content, the visual design often suffers.

Say, for instance, that a comp is designed for a list of recipes. Once a client has the keys to the site turned over to them, they may start adding or removing content, so a design that called for four recipes to be displayed on a page now has eight. Or perhaps the design allows for a recipe title that's 80 characters long, and the client decides to upload a title that's 200 characters long, causing the text to overlap its container. There are a myriad of ways a developer can fix these problems, but wouldn't it be more effective to change the way you work so your sites have the fluidity they need to accommodate these sorts of problems before they arise?

In a sense, the responsive web is about building for these sorts of factors as well. It's about building websites that are versatile, agile, and driven by purpose. The main purpose of a site is the content it contains, and a well-designed site is one that beautifully contextualizes and provides accessibility to that content.

That's why style guides are so important. They allow you to talk about the visualization of the site without having to solve the problem of contextualizing the content at the same time. How many times have you been designing a page and had a client change their mind about what certain navigation items should be called? Those problems shouldn't be dealt with when you're trying to establish a visual style for a site; they can more easily be resolved in a discussion about the specific labels and content that the site will have.

3.1.1 What is a style guide?

A *style guide* is a document used to communicate the design standards in place for the site being developed. It needs to communicate layout, branding, typography, color, and navigation to the team. With such a starting point as a guideline for the site design, designers can create a high-quality responsive site quickly and easily.

Most front-end developers spend the majority of their time looking for patterns in order to increase efficiency. A developer who is skilled at finding and capitalizing on visual patterns can dramatically reduce the time it takes to build a site. A style guide is a type of deliverable that gives developers these patterns in no uncertain terms.

When I was a kid, I loved *Highlights* magazine, a little, paper, bimonthly magazine that had cartoons and games in it. One of the games was called "Spot the Difference." You would be presented with two different drawings and asked to identify the difference between them. Being a front-end developer involves a lot of this—spotting the differences between comps, or between the site and the comp. The style guide is a sort of bible that developers can follow when executing a site.

Let's look at what's included in a style guide.

LAYOUT

When drafting a style guide, you want to make sure you specify spacing with a grid system. The grid may need to be altered for small and midsized screens, but it should give a general sense of proportion and spacing. A defined layout structure lets the developer know that grid blocks should have a certain width, padding, and margin.

BRANDING, PATTERNS, AND COLOR

Your style guide should say something about the client's online brand. This is more to show patterns and themes than anything else. Setting a color palette gives the team certain colors to work with, as opposed to having random combinations of colors and textures throughout the design.

TYPOGRAPHY

The typefaces used on a site are key to the overall site design. You'll want to indicate all typographic decisions as clearly as possible. Font sizes are relative, but font faces, weights, and styles are important information that should be communicated up front. Most clients have an established typeface, which is important to specify, but there are also other typefaces that may fit well within the project. It's also important to specify typographic decisions such as how large the base header or paragraph text should be and any inline text styling that will be used, such as italics or inline link styles.

NAVIGATION

Navigation applies specifically to user interface patterns and shapes. This means designing buttons, link styling, and iconography. Again, by pulling the design for these individual elements out of specific use cases, it opens the design up for consistency and lets you focus on how each element plays into the whole picture.

3.1.2 Developing a style guide

A style guide can be reverse-engineered when a site is being developed, but that's a bit backward. It's much like building a house so you can draft a blueprint. Instead, you can use style tiles, a framework for building style guides that has emerged in recent years. Whereas a mood board, or collection of images, might be too abstract, and a full page comp might be too absolute, style tiles enable designers to present just enough information without restricting a project. It's a good starting point for designers who need to present something to clients and developers so that the entire team can have a meaningful conversation about a site's visual design.

3.1.3 Style tiles: creating a visual language

Samantha Warren, the creator of style tiles (shown in figure 3.1), was in search of a way to provide her clients with a better deliverable. Traditional web design involves creating comps in Photoshop, and it can be, at times, an unsatisfying experience.

The problem with comps is that they tell too much about how a site is supposed to look, while not doing much to satisfy some of the most important aspects of a design. Although what a site looks like is important, so are what it does, how it loads, and what the experience feels like. To design a comp and then reproduce it in code is to apply your creativity to what I call a "dead end deliverable." A comp has no use once it's been sliced into pieces and put back together with code by a developer. A style tile doesn't resolve all these problems, but it's much quicker to assemble than a comp, and it can present a set of visual rules that define how a site should look, feel, and interact.

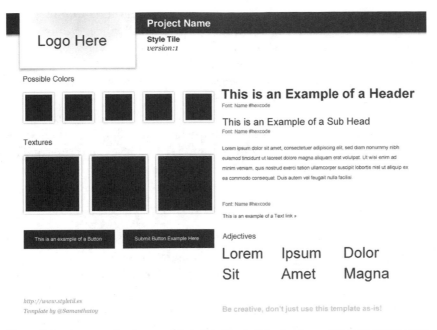

Figure 3.1   An example of an unstyled style tile. In this chapter, you'll learn how to turn this into a valuable asset that can communicate a site's design clearly and quickly.

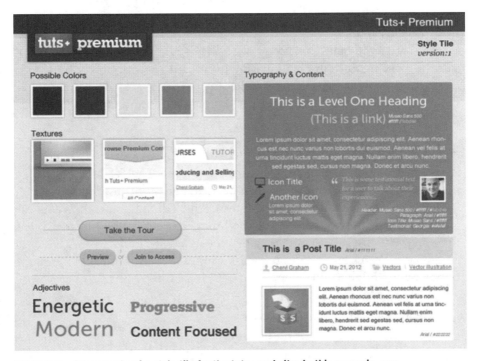

Figure 3.2   An example of a style tile for the tuts+ website. In this example, you can clearly see the core ideas behind the site's design start to come together.

With responsive design, a site can be built with meaningful deliverables. A rapid prototype guides a site's back-end structure. A style tile influences front-end design and can be used to offer design guidance as a site expands.

In her article in *A List Apart*, "Style Tiles and How They Work" (http://alistapart .com/article/style-tiles-and-how-they-work), Warren says that by relying on style tiles to inform design, she's able to have meaningful conversations with stakeholders about a site's visual elements earlier, without having to flesh out the entire layout of a site. This provokes thought and dialogue about what the client likes and how the client envisions the appearance of the site. The point is to achieve the results quickly without investing a large amount of time and energy too early in the process. Figure 3.2 shows what a completed style tile could look like.

3.2   How to create a style tile

Using style tiles as an early deliverable requires a huge amount of adaptation from every member of the team. It's not a burden that falls on the shoulders of the designer alone; rather, it requires all team members to shift the way they discuss the project and the project's visual identity.

Steve Jobs once said of Apple's design process that design isn't just how a thing looks, but how it feels. In order for internal teams to find success with something like a style tile, everyone needs to understand that they're building toward the goal of how a product is going to feel. Style tiles provide context for the product being built, but in order for them to work, teams have to hold off on the immediate urge to solve all of the problems at once.

So how do you build something that conveys not just a look, but also a feeling? You start by focusing on your client, having meaningful conversations, and learning from them. Next, you create a palette based on the feedback you received. This palette includes not just colors and typefaces, but adjectives and emotive terms to describe the projected end product.

3.2.1   Get feedback

Before starting on a style tile, it's crucial to get feedback about how a client defines their visual brand. Much of the design work that goes into a style tile depends on feedback from and direct interaction with the client. This might begin as a mood board or a collection of images that convey the brand's mood in the browser, but ultimately these mood boards are too vague to be used as a deliverable.

As part of a design kickoff survey, ask a series of questions to get at what your client is looking for. Some good examples of questions would be

- If your site was a soda, what would it be (for example, Coca-Cola Classic, Mountain Dew, Dr. Pepper)?
- Is your site modern or traditional?
- If your site was a city, what city would it be?

Ideally, you want to collect a series of adjectives to describe the site design. In this chapter, we'll design a blog you started work on in chapter 1 (see figure 1.8). If I were the client for this site, I might describe what I wanted from the site with adjectives like *rugged, industrial, artisan,* or *handcrafted.* I'd say that if my site was a beer, it would be Shiner Bock, because I want it to have a vintage, unique feel, but still appeal to a large audience. I'd probably describe it as simple and modern, but also somewhat rustic.

Once you know the direction your client wants to go, it's on to the palette.

3.2.2 Design the style tile

As with all frameworks, the format for designing style tiles is intended as a starting point. The base Photoshop file can be downloaded from http://styletil.es, but it can seem a bit bland (see figure 3.3).

This base gives you a roadmap for the asset you'll create. In it you have spaces for colors, textures, buttons, some type treatment, and a set of adjectives to describe the online brand of the client. There's also space to define a logo treatment and to document the name and version of the creative design standards being worked on.

You'll also notice the cyan vertical rules in the template. This grid layer gives a sense of the basic grid layout and relative sizing. It's most useful as a guide for the grid system in development. Most of the work here is intended to offer talking points and direction, so keep that in mind.

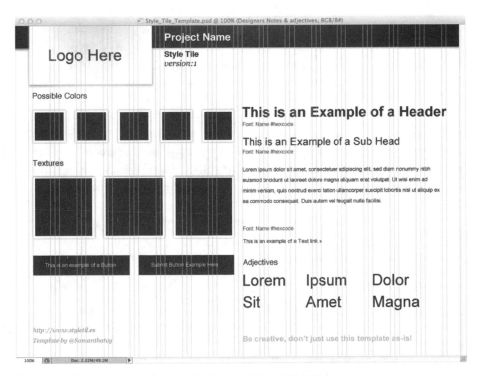

Figure 3.3   The base style tile, downloaded from http://styletil.es

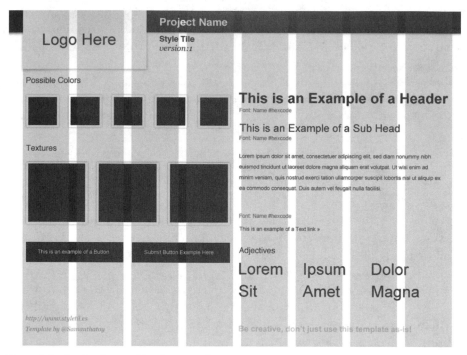

Figure 3.4   An 8-column grid using a semi-transparent red layer

The default is a 16-column grid, but feel free to adjust it to fit your site's needs. The blog that we'll design in this chapter will be a type-heavy site, so 16 columns might be too fine a standard. We'll adjust this and work with a simpler 8-column grid (figure 3.4).

In the previous chapter, we walked through the design of a mobile site and made some creative decisions, such as choosing the font families for this style tile. With the grid in place, you can start adding some already defined assets, such as the logo and some colors and typefaces. This is as simple as changing the swatches and placeholder text in the style tiles template file to ones that are brand-appropriate and that reflect the creative direction of the site.

In the style tile you're free to conceptualize the brand identity and interactive elements without having to create layout and infrastructure at the same time. This lets you focus on the important parts of the design and leads to better feedback from clients.

3.2.3   *Creating the style tile*

In order for your style tile to speak to the design of a site, you'll want to add some important elements. You should feel free to use your creativity to make the style tile unique to your project.

In figure 3.5, I've selected a typeface and added some texture, accent images, buttons, and adjectives to describe the site.

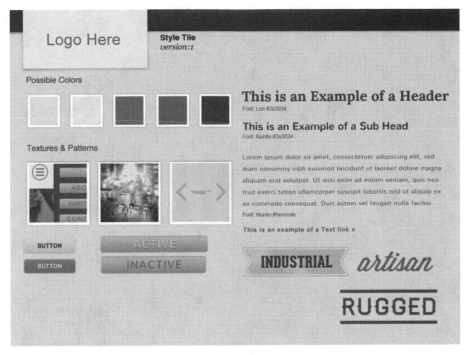

Figure 3.5   An early initial pass at creating a style tile

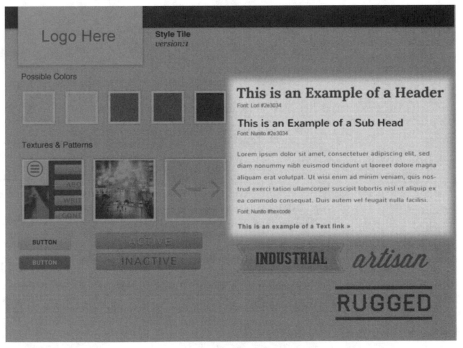

Figure 3.6   The typography portion of the style tile. The header font family is set to *Lori*, and subheads and body to font family *Nunito*.

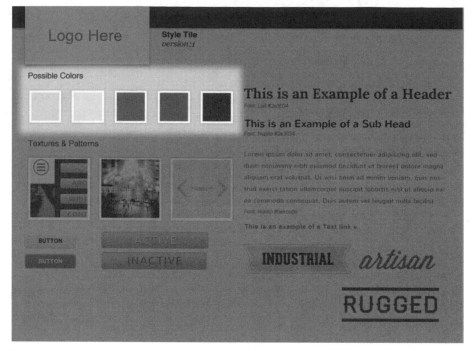

Figure 3.7   An example color swatch

TYPOGRAPHY

Adding type to the right side gives you a place to identify typographic style, as seen in figure 3.6. Font sizes, colors, weights, leading, and kerning can all be played with here to get a nice balance and articulate an idea.

COLORS

The color swatches on the style tile, highlighted in figure 3.7, present a small color palette that can be used in the site. These colors can be for text, call-to-action buttons, divider lines, accent points, and things like that. It's a base of colors for use in the site design.

By identifying the colors outside of the comps, you can better ensure consistency and find a unified palette. A site's color palette can become fractured if it's reverse-engineered from a comp; with a style tile, all colors are established before they're applied to the final site.

TEXTURES AND PATTERNS

Textures and patterns are nice to include in a style tile. Texture can be a useful design tool for separating levels of content or separating elements on a common plane. It's

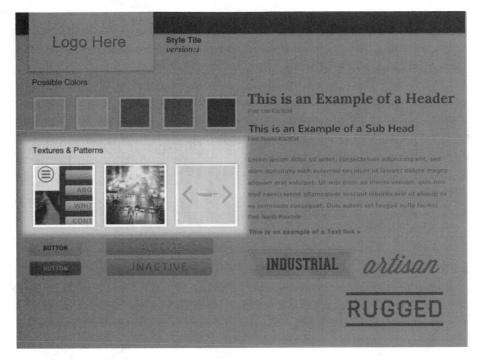

Figure 3.8 The "textures" here are little artifacts that capture some of the look and feel we want in the final product.

not a must-have, especially with flat design becoming more popular, but it's something that I like to plan with in some of my designs. In this area you can present free-form concepts that should end up in the final site.

Say, for instance, you have a site with a main content area with sections of callouts or elements that are tangential to the central content's focus. Textures give you a way to distinguish between these elements. You also might want a texture to fill your site's negative space and add more personality to the site.

For me, this section, shown in figure 3.8, is more of a mood board than anything else. The treatment of the images will translate into the final site, and the images themselves will inform the look and feel of the media used on the site.

BUTTONS

For buttons, shown in figure 3.9, you want to design something that looks clickable and that follows some accepted user interface standards. Your buttons don't always have to look glossy and rounded; what's important is that they contrast with the background and are obviously buttons.

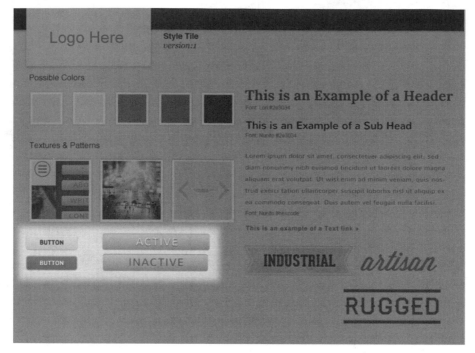

Figure 3.9   The buttons shown here communicate how they will look on the site, in terms of size, color, background contrast, typography, and so on.

Designer insight: user interface standards

Accepted user interface standards will depend on the company that produces them, but they're usually similar, like the iOS iPhone Human Interface Guidelines by Apple[a] and the design library for Windows Phone by Microsoft.[b]

---

[a]   Apple, "iOS Human Interface GuDo not, I'll do it manually.idelines," https://developer.apple .com/library/ios/documentation/userexperience/conceptual/mobilehig/MobileHIG.pdf.

[b]   Microsoft, "Design library for Windows Phone," http://msdn.microsoft.com/en-US/library/ windowsphone/design/fa00461b-abe1-41d1-be87-0b0fe3d3389d(v=vs.105).aspx.

ADJECTIVES

The adjectives section, shown in figure 3.10, should be more or less a playground for ideas. Use a few words to describe the visual brand and some typefaces to accentuate those points. The type and colors presented here don't necessarily have to be implemented in the final design; their purpose is to help articulate the end goals of the site to the client.

Once you've finished adding these elements, you've finished your style tile, and you have a base to start with. Keep in mind that the style tile is being built as a deliverable alongside the prototype. This reduces the need to create what I call "snapshot comps," which are only useful in showing one website state at a time.

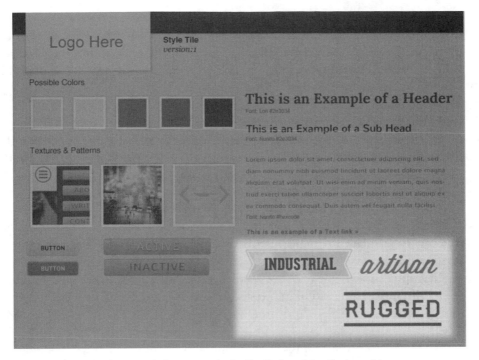

Figure 3.10   Adjectives can help communicate the final goal to clients and teams.

3.2.4   *Iterative design with a style tile*

Another great thing about style tiles is that they're easy to develop iteratively. You can start with multiple style tiles, each with unique design directions, and easily combine, revise, and add to them to create the final look and feel of the site.

Because style tiles focus on the parts of the design that matter, they can be produced quickly. A few designers can work on different directions independently, and each direction could reflect a different treatment of the user interface elements, mood boards, or colors. Each tile reflects a different impression of the client's brand, and each one could lead to different and fruitful conversations.

As you work through rounds of revisions, moving toward the final design direction, a style tile can be improved upon to develop the final design. I recommend setting a limit on the number of iterations, though, because criticizing visual elements is very easy, and ultimately the design will be integrated into a prototype that might cause the client and design team to rethink some of the style tile decisions.

3.3   *The death of the mockup*

Within the web design industry, there has been a lot of talk about what responsive web design means for the creation of Photoshop comps or mockups. If creating a mockup for every viewport is too labor intensive, and you use a style tile to identify visual style, where does this leave the traditional mockup?

This is a hard question to answer, and one I struggle with on a daily basis. For some traditional clients, mockups are a requirement. These clients are afraid of doing anything related to "coding" before they feel familiar with what they're buying. Many clients find technology intimidating, and are more comfortable with a PDF full of JPEGs. Other clients want everything in the browser as soon as possible. A balance is required.

Most clients (even traditional ones) can be won over to browser-based prototypes. It's all about using familiar terms to describe new ideas. For instance, I like to refer to rapid prototypes without any visual style as "high fidelity prototypes." I explain to the client that engaging with the site concept in the browser will give us feedback about the way they interact with it. Because everyone interacts with their devices a little differently, this is a great way to discover how your client interacts with their sites.

Mockups or comps are a poor deliverable for the development team. There's no true way to simulate a responsive environment (currently) with graphic design tools. In some projects, you could spend hours trying to figure out minor problems, like how a swipe should behave or how an object should follow a touch. Something as simple as binding an interaction to the start or the end of a touch can make or break the way an interaction feels. Unfortunately it's not possible to simulate that in a static design.

What does this mean for designers? Should every designer learn to code? No, coding and designing are two entirely different things, and there should be a division of labor between code and comp, if only because it's more economically viable. Having one person build an entire site's design *and* code is just too risky. It's extremely rare to find a developer who is a talented designer or a designer who is a talented coder. The two skillsets are very different and require unique ways of thinking.

What works best is collaborating closely with developers and designers. On one of my current projects, I sit next to the designer and we offer each other feedback as we create elements. He'll draft a module or component for the site, and I'll build it into the site templates, module by module.

So is the mockup dead? Yes and no. I think clients and designers still need some mockups, but ultimately how a site feels in the browser needs to supersede everything. A mockup can serve as a good target, and a style tile is great for filling in gaps. But don't spend too much time building mockups to figure out a site's details in the browser. Homepage or critical page mockups can be helpful, but the site prototype on the browser is where you can really explore every element of the design.

3.4   *Summary*

Designing based on style guides is a completely different approach from traditional web design. Responsive web design requires you to rethink a lot of the ways you go about building and designing websites. By abstracting the visual design from the layout and function of a site, you can produce a more specific deliverable, the style tile, that focuses on the immediate needs of a client.

Presenting design guidelines in the form of a style tile also offers designers a reprieve from repeating the same elements over and over again through various compositions, and having to maintain consistency between them. By using style tiles, you focus on what's most important to a designer: the design.

In the next chapter, we'll discuss some design patterns that you can use to implement navigation in responsive environments.

3.5 Discussion points

- How could you improve your process to facilitate better collaboration between designers and developers?
- What are some pain points in the design and development process? How do you think you could make the process easier?
- When designing a site, how do you try to anticipate how the site will look in the browser?
- When building the site, what do you do when you find something that won't work?

Responsive user
experience design patterns

4

This chapter covers

- The origins and importance of design patterns
- Using two different design patterns to solve the same problem

The architect Christopher Alexander is famous for his theories on the use of patterns in design, and his work has influenced software developers since the late '60s in various areas such as language design and modular programming.[1] His greatest influence has been on the development of software design patterns, popularized by Gamma, Helm, Johnson, and Vlissides in their 1995 book *Design Patterns*.[2] In building architecture, a design pattern is a way of documenting recurring problems and their solutions. In responsive design, design patterns help you avoid mistakes you've made in the past and establish familiar solutions to the common problems of web development.

---

[1] Nikos Salingaros, "Some Notes on Christopher Alexander," http://mng.bx/ZUdO.

[2] Erich Gamma, Richard Helm, Ralph Johnson, and John Vlissides, *Design Patterns: Elements of Reusable Object-Oriented Software* (Addison-Wesley Professional, 1995).

It would be impossible to list and create examples in this chapter for every responsive design pattern, primarily because these solutions are still being discovered, but also because doing so would fill an entire book.[3] Instead, I've opted to present two design patterns for navigation to show you how different solutions can achieve similar results. We'll focus on navigation because we already established a navigation design pattern in chapter 2 (the off-canvas design pattern), and also because it's a complex problem with multiple solutions.

It's important to explore the flexibility of the web and find accessible solutions to the specific challenges raised by your sites, so let's do that before we go forward with building the site in HTML and CSS.

Designer insight: user experience and site navigation

This chapter covers some elements directly related to the user's experience of a site. In some workplaces, you may have a specialist in user experience design. But whether you do or not, user experience is ultimately the responsibility of everyone involved in the project.

Navigation design is a very broad subject, and although the following chapters will present a few ways to approach it in a responsive site, educating yourself on the discipline of user experience is a good idea. A great starting resource is the book *Don't Make Me Think!*, Second Edition, by Steve Krug (New Riders, 2005).

Developer insight: why build from scratch

Earlier I used Foundation to build a navigation prototype, but here we're building one from scratch. Why? The reason for this is simple—every site is unique.

When I was a kid in shop class, my teacher taught me to use every saw in the room. Each saw had its own uses and added its own flair to a cut. By learning my tools and their uses, I expanded my ability to create. If you don't diversify your toolset, you can't diversify the kind of work you produce, and you begin to limit your creativity.

It's easy to use a framework and make it work for the design you've been given; I've had to do that on multiple projects, mostly when time was an issue. But in most of my work, clients have a unique problem or need, and they come to me to solve it. Ultimately, knowing what's going on under the hood will give you more control over what you can build. Conversely, depending on a third-party framework will limit the kind of work you can do. To become a mature and well-rounded front-end developer, you have to break free of your dependency on frameworks.

---

[3] A list of responsive design patterns can be found on This Is Responsive: http://bradfrost.github.io/this-is-responsive/patterns.html.

HOME   ABOUT   PRODUCTS   CONTACT

Figure 4.1   An example of a site's top-level navigation

4.1   *Single-level navigation*

Typically, sites are navigated through a series of links or buttons that sit at the very top of a web page. Top-level navigation commonly serves as a portal throughout the site. *Single-level* refers to the fact that there's no hidden or secondary navigation; there's only one level of navigation (Home, About, Products, and Contact in figure 4.1).

The problem with this in a responsive site is that the links and logos could get broken up and jumbled when displayed on a phone or tablet. In chapter 2, we talked about using off-canvas navigation to solve this sort of problem, but that isn't the only solution. Off-canvas navigation is a very common pattern and gives you some flexibility in adding layers to your horizontal spacing, but it can also be limiting; hiding all of the navigation for a site behind a toggle button introduces a single point of failure within the user experience. In spite of these shortcomings, it remains the dominant solution for responsive layouts due to its versatility and ease of use.

Designer insight: taking advantage of vertical space

One of the obvious reasons for using off-canvas navigation is to add some functionality to the very top of a page. This is useful because of the limited horizontal space in a mobile environment. Horizontal space is one of the defining characteristics of small screens; in development, we commonly set media queries strictly against the site's width.

There's an old publishing term that used to get thrown around a lot in web development: "above the fold." It's a reference to newspapers, where the top story and most expensive ad space are above the fold on the front page. If an article was really good or an advertiser paid the right price, that content would be placed above the fold.

In web design, this "above the fold" space manifested as the space on a page that's visible without scrolling. This screen real estate has been prized and has led to the trend of placing a carousel module in this space, so that more content can claim to be above this metaphorical fold. Unfortunately, the fold is a myth. In reality, content below the fold is viewed a great deal more than content in the second slide of a carousel.

According to ClickTale, a heatmap service provider, users scrolled 76% of pages with a scroll bar, and 22% were scrolled all the way to bottom.[a] WeedyGarden reports that if a home page carousel is clicked, the first slide is clicked 84% of the time and the remaining clicks are split between the other slides.[b]

[a]   "Unfolding the Fold," ClickTale blog, http://mng.bz/8nBx.

[b]   Erik Runyon, "Carousel Interaction Stats," WeedyGarden, http://weedygarden.net/2013/01/carousel-stats/.

> **(continued)**
>
> Web design offers many unique opportunities, but one of the less exploited is the availability of vertical space. A site has, literally, unlimited vertical space, but horizontal space is always dependent on the width of the browser window and is always a finite resource. Take advantage of this vertical space. Users will scroll down if your site looks good and loads quickly. Every meaningful visitor is there for a reason, and they'll be happy to explore your site if there's good content and a beautiful structure.

To solve the problem of top-level navigation in responsive design, let's focus on a couple of design patterns: toggle navigation and select menu. After we look at these patterns, we'll discuss the benefits and challenges of these two approaches and then move on to multilevel integration.

4.1.1 The toggle navigation pattern

The toggle navigation pattern is a method of displaying all of the top-level navigation below a menu button on smaller screens. The navigation toggles between the collapsed, inactive state and the expanded, active state when you tap the menu button. A good example of this can be seen on Starbucks.com, as shown in figure 4.2.

In single-level navigation, the menu on the desktop will mirror our earlier example in chapter 2. In a small-screen environment, the navigation will appear simply as a logo and a Menu button, with the content immediately below. Once the Menu button is tapped, the navigation expands downward and pushes the content further down.

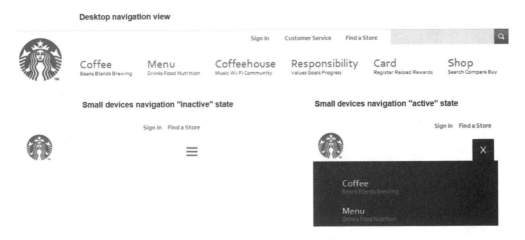

Figure 4.2   The responsive navigation on Starbucks.com

Figure 4.3 shows a mockup of the default (collapsed) and expanded states. The default state is what you'd see when the page is first displayed. The expanded state is what you'd see after tapping on the Menu button.

This design pattern has advantages in design as well as in development. As a design feature, this navigation is consistent in feel with the desktop version. The user looks to the same area for navigation in both desktop and mobile layouts, but because the navigation in the mobile layout is toggled behind a menu button, it has a smaller footprint. For the developer, this toggle navigation is easier to implement than some of the other navigation design patterns.

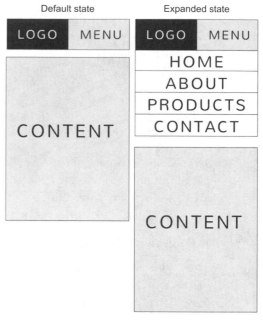

Figure 4.3   A small-screen toggle navigation menu. On the left is the default, collapsed, "inactive" state; on the right is the expanded "active" state.

CODING THE TOGGLE NAVIGATION

To code the toggle navigation, we'll use some HTML, CSS, and a little jQuery to toggle the expanded active state. First, here's the HTML, which can be found in the source code, in the 4.1 directory:

```
<header>
  <div id="logo" class="l-half grey">Logo</div>
  <div id="menu" class="l-half light-grey">Menu</div>
</header>
<nav id="nav">
  <ul>
    <li>Home</li>
    <li>About</li>
    <li>Products</li>
    <li>Contact</li>
  </ul>
</nav>
<article>
  <h2>Headline</h2>
    <p>Lorem ipsum ...</p>
</article>
```

The menu button will toggle the navigation state from inactive to active.

This is the navigation that will be hidden and shown when the navigation state toggles.

This is some strictly bare-bones markup. By default, we'll hide the navigation; we'll reveal it if the class of is-expanded is applied. We'll even animate it a little with a CSS transition. CSS transitions can help sell the effect of hiding and revealing the interface and give the user a little more context:

```css
* {
    text-transform: uppercase;
    font-family: Helvetica;
    text-align: center;
}
header, nav {
    width:100%;
}
ul {
    list-style: none;
    margin:0;
    padding:0;
    float:left;
    width:100%;
}
li {
    border-bottom: 1px solid #2e3034;
    margin:0;
    padding:20px 0;
    float:left;
    width:100%;
}

.l-half {
    width:50%;
    float:left;
    padding: 20px 0;
}
.grey {
    background:#2e3034;
    color:#fff;
}
.light-grey{
    background:#e4e4e4;
    color:#2e3034;
    outline:1px solid #2e3034;
}

nav {
    height:1px;
    overflow: hidden;
    width:100%;
    outline:1px solid #2e3034;
    -webkit-transition: height 1s;
}
nav.is-expanded {
    height:235px;
}
```

Boilerplate CSS rules provide basic styling.

By default, the navigation is I px tall with the overflow hidden.

This class will make the navigation visible.

Now add a media query to remove the Menu button and display the navigation. This code can be found in the 4.2 directory:

```
@media(min-width:700px){
    #logo {
        width:200px;
    }
    #menu {
        display: none;
    }
    nav, nav.is-expanded {
        height:60px;
        width:500px;
        float: right;
    }
    ul {
        width: 500px;
    }
    li{
        width:25%;
    }
    article {
        float:left;
    }
}
```

This toggle navigation helps move relevant content up to the top of the page on an initial page load, so the page's content takes priority and the user doesn't have to scroll through navigation items. In a desktop view, the navigation returns to being fully visible and accessible.

This approach has the benefit of keeping the navigation isolated at the top of the page, so if more elements are added, the layout doesn't break. It relies on a little bit of jQuery, but it could be converted easily to plain JavaScript to eliminate the need for a framework.

Here's what it looks like using jQuery (a demo can be viewed in the 4.3 directory):

```
$('#menu').click(function(){
  $('nav').toggleClass('is-expanded');
});
```

And here's the JavaScript equivalent for modern browsers that support the standard addEventListener method (there's a demo in the 4.4 directory):

```
document.getElementById('menu').addEventListener('click', function(){
  var el = document.getElementById('nav');
  el.className = el.className + 'is-expanded';
},false );
```

One of the biggest benefits of toggle navigation is that it easily scales up for a second level of navigation. This is useful if you have a complex site that requires a level of nested navigation; for instance, your site might have subpages within one section. Later in this chapter, we'll look at an example of how you can build multilevel navigation with the toggle navigation pattern.

Toggle navigation is one way to solve the problem of responsive navigation. It's great because it maintains a single codebase and can be rearranged to fit mobile and desktop environments. The biggest shortcoming of toggle navigation is that it limits the number of elements you can have in the top levels. I find this pattern to be most useful in sites with a small content management system (CMS), like a WordPress blog or a small personal site.

It's a good idea to keep your top-level navigation direct and simple, but in a very complex site, such as an e-commerce site or a large-scale online magazine, toggle navigation becomes too limiting. In these cases, a combination of off-canvas navigation and toggle navigation can be successful, but in large-scale sites it's crucial to evaluate the needs of the specific site before making a decision.

Another design pattern that helps solve the problem of responsive navigation is the select menu pattern.

4.1.2 The select menu pattern

The select menu pattern is one of the oldest responsive navigation design patterns; it provides simple interaction in a small space. This solution benefits the user in the same way that toggle navigation does, by reducing the vertical space the navigation occupies. When this navigation is triggered, the user engages with the browser's default select menu interface.

Our goal is to create a single level of navigation in a mobile environment. When we scale down to the mobile viewport, we'll see something a little different from the toggle navigation pattern. Here we'll have a `<select>` dropdown list in place of a menu, as shown in figure 4.4.

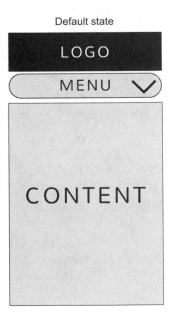

Figure 4.4 A small-screen select menu. On the left is the collapsed state; on the right is the expanded, active state (using the iOS 5 default for the select menu).

CODING THE SELECT MENU NAVIGATION

The code for the select menu navigation will be similar to the previous toggle navigation pattern, but instead of changing the format of the navigation code and hiding the menu, we'll hide and show a select menu. The code for this is in the 4.5 directory.

Our header markup will look like this:

```
<header>
  <div id="logo" class="1-half grey">Logo</div>
  <select id="menu">
    <option value="">Menu</option>
    <option value="/home">Home</option>
    <option value="/about">About</option>
    <option value="/practice">Products</option>
    <option value="/contact">Contact</option>
  </select>
</header>
```

In menu, the value attribute will be the destination URL. Imagine that each option tag is an anchor; the href in the anchor would be the value in the option menu.

In the browser, this will do nothing by itself, so we need a little jQuery to make this work:

```
$("#menu").change(function onChange() {
  window.location = $(this).find("option:selected").val();
});
```

With this little touch of jQuery, the user can navigate deeper into the site. The change method listens for the menu to change status and runs the onChange event handler once the event has taken place.

The main benefit of this pattern is that it uses a minimal amount of JavaScript. It saves space and uses the operating system's user interface to display the navigation. This pattern is valuable when you're dealing with a large number of links.

4.1.3 *Toggle navigation versus select menu*

There are several benefits and drawbacks to each of these design patterns. The toggle navigation pattern is effective at masking navigation elements and saving space in a small screen, but it suffers from a lack of versatility. The select menu is also compact and to the point, but it is, to be honest, a huge hack.

These are the immediate drawbacks of the select menu:

- It depends 100% on the browser's support of JavaScript. If there's no JavaScript, the user will be completely stuck.
- Select menus can be brutal to style across different browsers, and the creative graphic design can be compromised by the default styling. You're very limited in your ability to control the presentation of the navigation.
- The select menu can't be refactored for desktop views. If the user scales up to a desktop view, the select menu is completely ineffective and should be replaced with a desktop menu.

Toggle navigation also has several drawbacks:

- Toggle navigation favors simplicity and can lack the depth required for complex navigation patterns. If your site has multiple tiers of navigation, that might be difficult to maintain with toggle navigation.
- Toggle navigation takes advantage of vertical space. If you're using a sticky header (you shouldn't be, as I'll explain shortly), the toggle navigation could end up getting cut off.

Developer insight: why you should avoid sticky headers

"The navigation should follow the user down the page. That way, if they need to move to another page, they can without scrolling up to the top." (This is a quote from a UX guy I used to know.)

Here's the problem with sticky headers: they take up too much space in mobile. I mentioned earlier how vertical space is an unlimited resource, but that's not true if things are fixed on the page. When something is fixed on the page, it's difficult to navigate around it, because its position is static. Fixed-size elements lack the fluidity required for changing viewports. The same problems start to arise when you apply a fixed position to anything on the page. When something is fixed, it's not responding to its environment. Avoid fixed elements at all costs. (Modal pop-ups, I'm looking at you.)

These two navigation patterns meet varied needs and can be useful in different situations. Ultimately, I think the select menu pattern is good to use in a pinch, until you figure out something better. Whenever possible, though, I try to use toggle navigation or the off-canvas navigation that you saw in section 2.2.1.

4.2 Multilevel toggle navigation

We've covered a couple of basic navigation patterns in this chapter, but sometimes you need multiple tiers of navigation. In a select menu, these can simply be listed along with the other navigation elements, so an example isn't very exciting, but toggle navigation can be expanded to accommodate a second tier, as shown in figure 4.5.

When you have a second tier in your navigation, you need to find ways to group navigation elements. In common desktop implementations, a navigation element is hovered over, and it reveals the second level of navigation. In a mobile implementation,

Figure 4.5   A desktop example of multilevel navigation

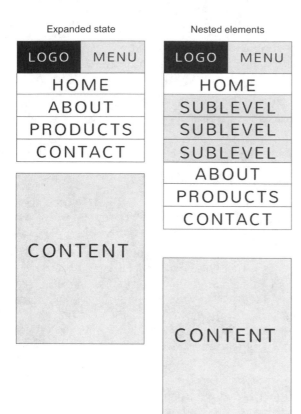

Figure 4.6   Toggle navigation with nested elements. On the left is the usual expanded menu; on the right, the user has expanded the navigation one level deeper by tapping on Home.

the second tier can be shown between its parent element and the parent's sibling, as you can see in figure 4.6.

In this figure, you can see an example of toggle navigation with a second tier. On the left, the navigation is one level deep, meaning that the user has expanded the menu using the Menu button. On the right, the user has expanded the navigation one level deeper by tapping on Home. This provides direct access to a subsection of pages.

CODING THE MULTILEVEL TOGGLE NAVIGATION

Here we have some HTML that displays a second menu level as an unordered list when its parent link is clicked. The code is available in the 4.6 directory:

```
<header>
  <div id="logo" class="l-half grey">Logo</div>
  <div id="menu" class="l-half light-grey">Menu</div>
</header>
<nav>
  <ul>
    <li class="has-subnav">
      <a href="#">Home</a>
      <ul class="subnav">
```

List element with a convenience CSS class that's used as a jQuery event hook for the links that will open the subnavigation

Subnavigation list with the CSS class subnav that hides the submenus by default

```
        <li><a href="#">sub-nav link</a></li>
        <li><a href="#">sub-nav link</a></li>
        <li><a href="#">sub-nav link</a></li>
        <li><a href="#">sub-nav link</a></li>
      </ul>
      </li>
      <li>
        <a href="#">About</a>
      </li>
      <li>
        <a href="#">Products</a>
      </li>
      <li>
        <a href="#">Contact</a>
      </li>
    </ul>
</nav>
<article>
  <h2>Headline</h2>
  <p>
    Lorem ipsum […]
  </p>
</article>
```

Subnavigation list items

Next, let's style the multilevel navigation with some CSS, hiding the nested menus by default styling the subnav class:

```
*{
  text-transform: uppercase;
  font-family: Helvetica;
  text-align: center;
}

header, nav{
width:100%;
}

ul{
  list-style: none;
  margin:0;
  padding:0;
  float:left;
  width:100%;
}
ul.subnav{
  height:0px;
  overflow:hidden;
}

li.is-expanded ul.subnav{
  height:236px;
}
```

CSS rules that provide basic styling.

.subnav hides all the subnavigation lists by default by setting a 0 px height.

.subnav height is increased (and shown) when a li (list item) parent is set with the CSS class of .is-expanded.

```
ul.subnav li a{
  background:#e4e4e4;
}

li a{
  border-bottom: 1px solid #2e3034;
  margin:0;
  padding:20px 0;
  float:left;
  width:100%;
}

.l-half{
  width:50%;
  float:left;
  padding: 20px 0;
}

.grey{
  background:#2e3034;
  color:#fff;
}

.light-grey{
  background:#e4e4e4;
  color:#2e3034;
  outline:1px solid #2e3034;
}
```

CSS rules that provide basic styling.

```
nav{
  height:1px;
  overflow: hidden;
  width:100%;
  outline:1px solid #2e3034;
  -webkit-transition: height 1s;
}
```

The whole navigation is hidden by setting its height to I px.

```
nav.is-expanded{
height:235px;
}
```

Navigation height will be increased when you add the class is-expanded.

```
nav.is-expanded.is-subnav-expanded{
  height:470px;
}
```

Navigation height will be increased more when subnavigation is shown.

The previous HTML and CSS will hide all the navigation at page load. In order to show the main navigation menu and subnavigation menus, you have to manipulate the navigation CSS classes with a little bit of JavaScript:

jQuery click event handler for the menu button (the one inside the header element).

```
$('#menu').click(function(){
  $('nav').toggleClass('is-expanded');
});
```

Add (or remove) the .is-expanded CSS class on the "nav" navigation element when the menu button is clicked.

jQuery click event handler for the links in the navigation menu that are descendants of a list item with the CSS class .has-subnav.

Add (or remove) CSS class .is-expanded on the list item parent of the clicked link element. This .is-expanded class is a state class that applies the expanded state styles to the li.

```
$('.has-subnav a').click(function(){
  $(this).parent().toggleClass('is-expanded');
  $('nav').toggleClass('is-subnav-expanded');
});
```

Add (or remove) the .is-subnav-expanded rule on the main navigation element. This rule will add more height to the "nav" element so the menus and submenus become visible.

It's important to limit the vertical space you're using without removing important pieces of data or resources in small devices. With this code, you can achieve responsive multi-tier navigation that can adapt to small-screen devices. It's yet another example of how you can adapt your sites to the responsive web.

4.3 Responsive user experience design pattern resources

As I mentioned at the beginning of the chapter, it's really difficult to list all the patterns in a single chapter, in part because new patterns are always emerging. Brad Frost maintains a good repository of responsive patterns at the This is Responsive website seen in figure 4.7 (http://bradfrost.github.io/this-is-responsive/patterns.html). This page provides an updated list of patterns that designers and programmers are using, classified by type: layout, navigation, images, media, forms, text, and modules (which are also called components in frameworks like Bootstrap).

The site also provides a comprehensive list of resources about responsive web design patterns (http://bradfrost.github.io/this-is-responsive/resources.html).

4.4 Summary

In this chapter, we've discussed responsive navigation patterns, and I've outlined two different approaches to top-level navigation in responsive designs. This is just the tip of the iceberg. There are patterns for page layouts, text elements, and modules, with new patterns being discovered and implemented every day.

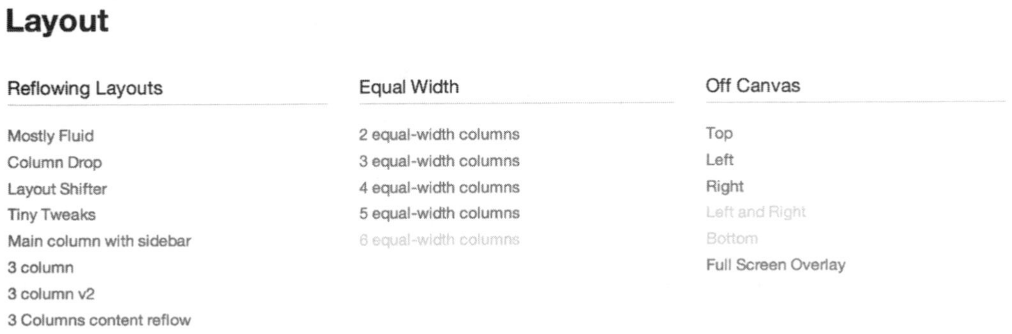

Layout

Reflowing Layouts	Equal Width	Off Canvas
Mostly Fluid	2 equal-width columns	Top
Column Drop	3 equal-width columns	Left
Layout Shifter	4 equal-width columns	Right
Tiny Tweaks	5 equal-width columns	Left and Right
Main column with sidebar	6 equal-width columns	Bottom
3 column		Full Screen Overlay
3 column v2		
3 Columns content reflow		

Figure 4.7 An example of the list of responsive patterns available at the This Is Responsive website

I've presented these two patterns simply to show you that there can be multiple solutions to the same problem. By exploring the variety of possibilities, you can build, not according to trends, but to meet the specific needs of your site.

When attempting to solve the problem of responsive navigation, it's important to keep the following questions in mind:

- What are the needs of this particular site? How is it going to be updated and how often?
- How can I take advantage of the space available in small-screen environments?
- Am I prioritizing the content and making sure the user has immediate access to what they came to this site for?

In the next chapter, we'll dive into building site layouts using percentages. You'll learn the fundamentals of working in percentages as opposed to using fixed-pixel layouts, and how to avoid making rigid websites.

4.5   Discussion points

- What commonly used web design patterns can you think of? For instance, this chapter deals with navigation, but what other patterns are frequently repeated in web design?
- When designing a site component that's commonly used, how much do you rely on a pattern and how much do you innovate?

Responsive layouts 5

This chapter covers

- Using percentages to create fluid layouts
- Animating the off-canvas navigation pattern
- Adjusting the layout for varied screen sizes

Building a responsive layout is, quite possibly, the easiest task in building a responsive website. All a layout has to do is gracefully refactor at given breakpoints. In chapter 1, I showed you some media queries to enable this refactoring, and you saw how selectors can override each other when applied from within a media query. To build a responsive layout, you just need to apply this logic. An element in a small screen should be one width, and then another width in a larger screen. But despite how simple this sounds, things always find a way of getting more complicated.

Responsive layouts tend to get more complicated because layout is often still determined in fixed terms. When a layout is created in a graphics editing program, the sizing is specified using measurements like pixels. It's easy to adjust sizes and share screen space when you're using CSS, but doing it in graphics programs is a recipe for inconsistency and extraneous coding because there's an inherent difference in the way these two technologies render their visual layers. That's why it's important to determine layout for a responsive site in the browser, not in a comp.

In this chapter, we'll cover the most effective ways of crafting a responsive layout. This means building a fluid grid system using percentages instead of pixels. We'll also cover some of the tricks you can use to make this process a little easier.

> **Designer insight: a designer's role in layout**
>
> Though much of the hands-on responsibility for layout lies on the shoulders of the developer, an art director's sense of space is absolutely crucial to prevent the layout from looking too static or uniform.
>
> Quick sketches and regular, short check-ins are crucial so that the designer retains input in this phase of the process. Naturally, this is going to require some understanding and trust on both sides, but the result of working like this is a site that everyone can be proud of.

5.1   *Fluid layouts via percentages*

In responsive web design, you'll notice the use of percentages for layout widths. These percentages create what's called a *fluid layout*, which is a layout that adjusts to the available space. In order to understand how this works and why it's important, you need to know how box sizing and percentages work in CSS.

5.1.1   *How percentages work in CSS*

Historically, web designs based all sizing on pixels. These pixels represent screen pixels, although it's not a one-to-one representation. High DPI screens will convert what's set as a "px" or "pixel" size into its appropriate grouping of screen pixels. This conversion can be complicated and isn't particularly important for our purposes; what is important is understanding that pixels are fixed units of measurement on digital screens. A pixel on a screen is a unit of measure, like a centimeter or an inch on a ruler.

The problem with pixel sizing in responsive web design is that a fixed size doesn't lend itself well to scaling. Once it's set, it's set. The elements set with pixels can have their sizes adjusted, but this requires changing everything on the screen. To effectively build a responsive site, you need to set sizes relative to something, and this is where percentages come into play.

Percentages work in CSS as you might expect: an element occupies a percentage of some space. That percentage of space is determined by the parent element. If a parent element is 1,000 pixels wide, and inside it are two elements, one of which is 20% wide and the other 80% wide, the element that's 20% wide will be rendered as 200 pixels wide and the one that's 80% wide will be rendered at 800 pixels wide. The total adds up to the 1,000-pixel-wide parent element (see figure 5.1).

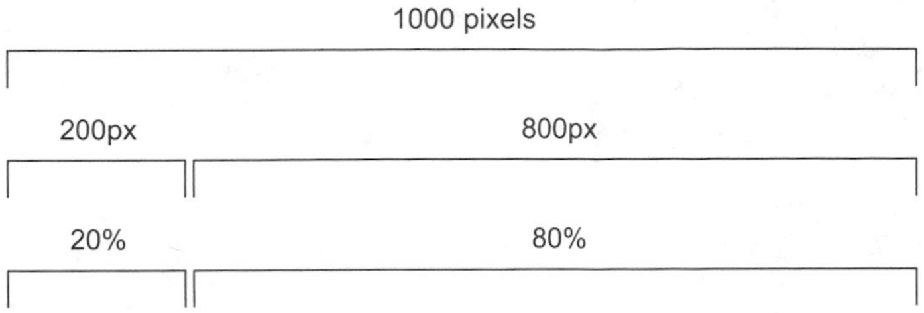

Figure 5.1   Widths represented in percentages

If figure 5.1 was represented in code, it might look like this (it's included in the 5.3 directory of this chapter's source code):

```
<div class="parent">
    <div class="twenty-percent">
    </div>
    <div class="eighty-percent">
    </div>
</div>
<style "type=text/css">
.parent{
    width:1000px;
    height:20px;
    outline:1px solid green;
}
.twenty-percent{
    width:20%;
    height:20px;
    float:left;
    background:red;
}
.eighty-percent{
    width:80%;
    height:20px;
    float:left;
    background:blue;
}
</style>
```

This code produces a 20-pixel-tall line:

When you scale this down in size, it can retain the same proportions. The layout remains "fluid" because it's relative to a fixed point on the page, in this case the parent (.parent) element. By using percentages, you've detached the layout from a fixed pixel width that's only useful in a single situation.

You can see this by changing the percentages to pixels in the example. Let's change the previous rules as follows:

```
.twenty-percent{
    width:200px;
    height:20px;
```

```
    float:left;
    background:red;
}
.eighty-percent{
    width:800px;
    height:20px;
    float:left;
    background:blue;
}
```

This code still creates this line (available in the 5.1 directory this chapter's source code):

The image is thicker because the line is a strict 1,000 px, but the width of the red and blue lines is the same. But watch what happens if you shrink the .parent element to 800 pixels wide:

```
.parent{
    width:800px;
    height:20px;
    outline:1px solid green;
}
```

The layout is now broken (available in the 5.2 directory):

The 800-pixel-wide element is too big to be in line with the 200-pixel element, and it has moved to a second line. But if you change the 200px and 800px back to percentages, you'll get a different result entirely:

```
.twenty-percent{
    width:20%;
    height:20px;
    float:left;
    background:red;
}
.eighty-percent{
    width:80%;
    height:20px;
    float:left;
    background:blue;
}
```

The line is now back in place, except it's 800 pixels wide instead of 1,000 pixels, because the two objects have kept their widths relative to their shared parent (viewable in the 5.3 source code):

At this point, you might say, "but there's still a fixed pixel size—the `.parent` element!" You'd be right, but this is just an example. In practice, that `.parent` element could be the browser's viewport. The point here is that you should keep everything relative, flexible, and fluid. Just as liquids fill the space they're given, so do fluid layouts.

Developer insight: what about height?

If you're paying attention, you might have noticed that I've been using fluid widths, but even in the examples here I used a pixel height. I set the height so the elements are visible, but fixed heights can often be troublesome; if their inner elements have a greater height, they can overlap the fixed-height element.

One way of overcoming this problem is to let the child elements determine their own height automatically. For example, if you need to set a height that's relative to the width of an element, such as to maintain aspect ratio, an effective way is to set the height to 0, and then use `padding-bottom` to set the proper percentage. This is because padding is set relative to the width of the parent element, just like width, and that also applies to padding on the top and bottom. Most browsers will still display the content if it's contained in the padding of an element.

We'll implement this technique (box sizing) in the following section.

5.1.2 Box sizing

Maintaining margins and padding is one of the things that makes responsive design very difficult. Say you have the previous 20% and 80% example, and you want to put some margin between the two elements. This would be easy if you had nice round numbers for your margin, like 1% or 2%. In a perfect world, you could just draw the 20%-wide box as 19%, add a `margin-left` of 1%, and be done with it.

Unfortunately this is rarely the case. In the real world, you'll find yourself searching for percentages that aren't that rounded. You could end up trying to use a `margin-left` of 1.5436%. You could easily do some math, subtract the padding from width, and adjust. But this becomes a real burden when you need `padding-left` and `padding-right`. Then you'll find that the padding needs some tweaking, and you'll have to change things over and over.

Fortunately, there's a better way. CSS3 introduced a property in CSS called `box-sizing`, and this property is used to alter the CSS box model. The typical box model width is determined by a simple sum, like this (where *width* is the width specified in the element):

padding-left + border-left + width + padding-right + border-right = total width

The initial value of `box-sizing` is `content-box`, and it implements the classic box-model equation above. By setting `box-sizing: border-box`, the width of an element is determined like this (where *rendered width* is the width specified in the element):

$width = rendered\ width$

Figure 5.2 shows this another way: two elements with the same defined width, left and right padding, and left and right borders but with different box-sizing. Even though both elements have the same width, the first box occupies more space because it's rendered with `box-sizing: content-box`, which, as you saw previously, is the sum of the specified width plus left and right borders and left and right padding. The box at the bottom is

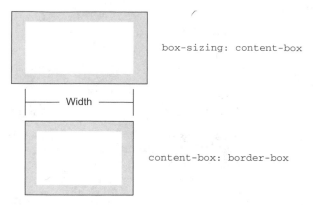

box-sizing: content-box

content-box: border-box

Figure 5.2   Two elements with the same width, padding, and borders but with different box sizing. The gray areas are the padding, and the black lines are the borders.

rendered with `content-box: border-box`. The rendered width of the box will be the specified width; the left and right padding and border space will be subtracted from the content space.

Let's create a working example that illustrates the box-sizing concept. Here's a simple grid of four 25% width elements, illustrated in figure 5.3 and viewable in the 5.4 directory of the source code:

```
<div class="grid"></div>
<div class="grid"></div>
<div class="grid"></div>
<div class="grid"></div>
```

```
.grid{
  width: 25%;
  height: 0px;
  padding-bottom: 25%;
  float: left;
  outline: 5px solid red;
}
```

Exactly 100%.

padding-bottom is used to give height to the divs (see the "what about height?" developer insight sidebar).

Add an outline to the four divs so we can easily identify them.

Figure 5.3   A simple grid

Everything is going just fine, but let's put some padding between these elements:

```
.grid{
  width:25%;
  height:0px;
```

```
  padding-left:1.5678%;
  padding-right:1.5678%;
  padding-bottom:10%;
  float:left;
  outline:5px solid red;
}
```

Add padding left and right to the divs to demonstrate how the initial box sizing works (content-box).

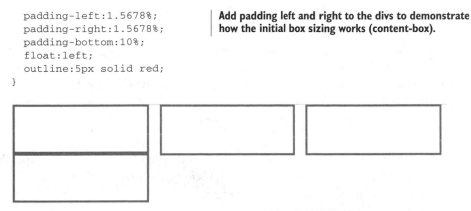

Figure 5.4   A broken grid. Applying `box-sizing` will fix this. (This is included in the 5.5 directory in the chapter 5 source code.)

Now, in figure 5.4, all of our spacing is off. Our grid is broken, but by changing the box-sizing property, we can change how the elements' widths and heights are calculated. By adding the following rule, you can set all the elements to use the `border-box` box-sizing model, as seen in figure 5.5:

```
*{box-sizing:border-box;}
```

The asterisk (*) universal selector is a CSS rule that will be applied to all the elements in the document.

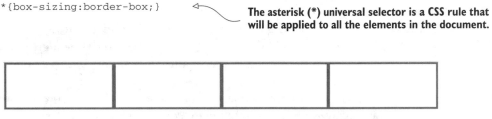

Figure 5.5   Now with `box-sizing` added. You can view this in the 5.5.1 directory in the chapter 5 source code.

Now you can change your padding to be whatever you want without affecting your grid! This will make building responsive sites dramatically easier by ensuring that sizing is predictable.

BROWSER SUPPORT   One concern with box-sizing might be browser support. Fortunately, box-sizing works in all modern browsers and Internet Explorer starting with IE8. Unfortunately, there's no fallback for IE7 and under, so if supporting IE7 and lower is a priority, you might be better off avoiding box-sizing altogether.

5.1.3   Fluid grid systems

Now that you know how fluid layouts work in a purely structural sense, let's talk about grid systems. Around the time that "Web 2.0" became a thing, web designers switched from using table-based layouts to div-based layouts, which created the need for a

div-based grid system, such as the hugely popular 960 grid system, found at http://
www.960.gs. The grid system was popularized as a method for applying vertical structure to a webpage. It arranged the site into columns to give more sense to the structure of the content.

Because of the predictable nature of screen sizes at the time, layout grids were set
at a standard size, like 1,024 pixels wide. Now this predictability has vanished, and an
alternative approach is required. Now we need a fluid grid system.

OUT OF THE BOX GRIDS

Many frameworks include grid systems out of the box. Bootstrap (http://
getbootstrap.com/) and Foundation both include their own unique grids, but they're
similar enough that when you're picking a front-end framework, the included grid
systems shouldn't be a deciding factor.

There are dozens of other self-contained grid systems, such as Skeleton and The
Golden Grid system. These too amount to a matter of taste and are nearly identical. I
refrain from using the out of the box grids most of the time, simply because in production you'll likely only ever use a small number of their features, and generally
you'll require a custom grid system with sizes that reflect the needs of the site. If a grid
does its job, it should be consistent throughout the site, so it's better to base the grid
on the design and maintain that grid's consistency.

BUILDING A GRID

In order to show how a basic grid system works, we'll build a grid rather than use an
out of the box fluid grid. We'll build a single "row" class to define a grouping of grid
pieces, a "grid" class to define a grid piece, and a few classes for the number of columns each grid should occupy.

First you need to identify how many columns you want each row to contain. For
the sake of simplicity, we'll start with an eight-column grid for the desktop and a four-
column grid for mobile, as seen in figure 5.6.

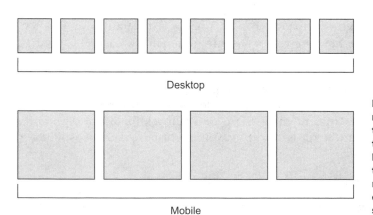

Desktop

Mobile

**Figure 5.6 Desktop and
mobile grids. It's important
that the number of columns in
the desktop grid be divisible
by the number of columns in
the mobile grid, so that the
rows contain an even number
of columns and the grid
structure is retained.**

To create an eight-column grid, we'll start with some boilerplate HTML and simple CSS. We'll make an eight-column row that breaks into four columns for mobile. We'll set the sizing against the grid elements as opposed to the row itself (which is a popular method in some "out of the box" grids). This gives us the flexibility to adjust the grid elements within the row.

Here's the HTML:

```
<div class="row">
  <div class="grid m-grid-1 d-grid-1">
  </div>
  <div class="grid m-grid-1 d-grid-1">
  </div>
  <div class="grid m-grid-1 d-grid-1">
  </div>
  <div class="grid m-grid-1 d-grid-1">
  </div>
  <div class="grid m-grid-1 d-grid-1">
  </div>
  <div class="grid m-grid-1 d-grid-1">
  </div>
  <div class="grid m-grid-1 d-grid-1">
  </div>
  <div class="grid m-grid-1 d-grid-1">
  </div>
</div>
```

And here's the CSS:

```
.row{
  width:100%;
  max-width:960px;
  /* for desktop view */
  margin:0 auto;
  outline: 1px solid blue;
  /* to visualize our element */

}

/* clearfix set against the row class  for convenience */
.row:before,.row:after {content: " ";display: table;}
.row:after {clear: both;}

.grid{
  height:20px;
  /* to visualize */
  float:left;
  margin:1%;
  outline:1px solid red;
  /* to visualize */
}

.m-grid-1{
  width:12.5%;
}
```

Apply the clearfix hack to the rows to prevent collapsing margins caused by contending float elements.

Set the width of a CSS rule that takes the space of one column in the grid.

```
@media (min-width:960px){
  .d-grid-1{width:10.5%;}
}
```

Set the width of the CSS rule for one column using a media query that targets devices with a minimum width of 960 pixels.

In figure 5.7 we have the beginnings of a custom fluid grid system. The elements here represent one row with eight columns inside; the blue and red border is to visualize the space that the columns will take. The classes prefixed with m- are for the mobile grid, and the classes prefixed with d- are for the desktop grid. Each object has its width applied by its m- or d- class.

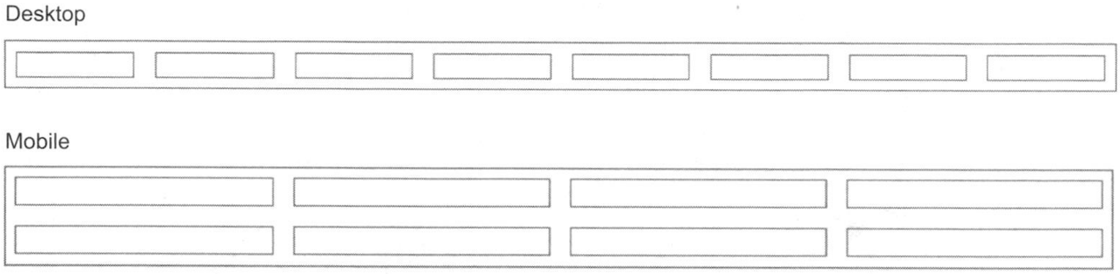

Desktop

Mobile

Figure 5.7   The start of a simple grid system with mobile and desktop views. You can view it in the 5.6 directory within the chapter 5 source code.

You can expand this grid system by adding more grid-sizing classes. (The grid created by the code can be viewed in the 5.7 directory within the chapter 5 source code.)

```
.m-grid-1{width:23%;}
.m-grid-2{width:48%;}
.m-grid-3{width:73%;}
.m-grid-4{width:98%;}
```

Rules that specify the width percentage for columns on the grid; a column with .m-grid-2 will take twice the space of a column with the rule .m-grid-I, and so on.

```
@media (min-width:960px){
  .d-grid-1{width:10.5%;}
  .d-grid-2{width:23%;}
  .d-grid-3{width:35.5%;}
  .d-grid-4{width:48%;}
  .d-grid-5{width:60.5%;}
  .d-grid-6{width:73%;}
  .d-grid-7{width:85.5%;}
  .d-grid-8{width:98%;}
}
```

Media query with breakpoint to min-width:960px specifies the size for grid columns for this screen size.

With these new rules, you now can build layouts with a bare-bones grid system. You can adjust it to fit your needs, but this should give you the underlying basis for building something more robust. The CSS class name for each column would be like this: *X-grid-Y. X* is replaced with either *m* for mobile or *d* for desktop; *Y* is a number from 1 through 8 representing the number of columns. You could potentially break this down further by adding a t- prefix for tablets and a second breakpoint.

This sort of fluid grid is helpful in creating a basic fluid layout, but let's dig into some trickier components.

5.2 *Building a fluid layout*

With the basics out of the way, it's time for us to dig in and build a layout. In this section we'll build a fluid, responsive header for our site that adapts to a fixed width in the desktop size. We'll build parts of the page that refactor themselves as they change viewports.

5.2.1 *Interpreting the prototype*

If we were pressed for time, we could develop straight from our prototype in chapter 1, but we aren't, so we'll break the prototype into pieces so we can identify all the parts, and then combine them into a whole. Building a layout out of a prototype is simply a matter of trying to find efficiencies and applying the design to the code you have.

Given that one prototype can be wildly different from the next, there's no set way to interpret a prototype. I can, however, give you a few tips to make it easier:

- A prototype is for communicating ideas—nothing in the prototype form is final. Remember this when you're interpreting what's in a prototype.
- Identify groupings of objects on the page to identify major layout components. This will help you determine the templates you need and identify the layout options you need to accommodate.
- The design elements in the prototype should serve to inform the typography and user interface. It's helpful to write the code for these layout elements and typographical design before you build the actual page. This can serve as a style guide for the site and encourage consistency between all the pages.

After you've identified your first layout elements, it's time to start coding. For our example site, we'll start with a header.

5.2.2 *Starting coding*

Browsers parse HTML first to determine DOM structure, so it's important to keep your markup as tidy as possible while writing code that's maintainable. Your markup is going to be interpreted by browsers as well as people, and a good front end should appeal to the interests of both. Dissecting how browsers work is too big a topic to cover here, but any time you spend reading up on the inner workings of web browsers will be time well spent.

Designer insight: inside the browser

Learning how browsers render web pages can be especially challenging for designers who don't spend time writing code and seeing how HTML and CSS interact. To learn more on the subject, take a look at Rob Crowther's great book, *Hello! HTML5 & CSS3* (Manning, 2012).

(continued)

Another good resource on the subject is the 2011 article by Tali Garsiel and Paul Irish, "How Browsers Work: Behind the scenes of modern web browsers" (http://www.html5rocks.com/en/tutorials/internals/howbrowserswork/), which is a revision of a previous publication by Garsiel.

Figure 5.8 shows what the header (with two placeholder red squares for buttons and the grey placeholder center block for a logo) will look like after we've written the markup and added CSS.

Figure 5.8   The header, with two buttons represented by red squares and a grey logo placeholder in the center, after we've written the markup and added CSS

Let's write some markup for the required elements to render figure 5.8 (code samples for this section can be found in the 5.8 directory of this chapter's source code). We'll need two text content areas: one for some supplemental information and one for navigation. In the markup, we also want the site to retain the same basic structure as the viewport expands.

```
<div class="wrapper">
  <header id="topHeader">
    <aside class="left-tray">
      <p>Brief bio [...]</p>
      <nav>
        <a href="#">Twitter</a>
        <a href="#">Github</a>
        <a href="#">Contact</a>
      </nav>
    </aside>
    <span id="infoTray"></span>
    <div class="logo"></div>
    <span id="navTray"></span>
    <aside class="right-tray">
      <nav>
        <a href="#">Home</a>
        <a href="#">About</a>
```

The aside tags will be used for off-canvas navigation in the mobile view.

The infoTray and navTray spans represent the two squares with red borders in figure 5.8.

```
        <a href="#">Writing</a>
        <a href="#">Contact</a>
      </nav>
    </aside>
  </header>
  <article></article>
</div>
```

The aside tags will be used for off-canvas navigation in the mobile view.

The markup for this section is pretty straightforward. We've taken the substance of the prototype and added some content and design to improve communication and ease of use. Now we need to add some CSS for layout.

Developer insight: layout versus style

CSS is used to add both styles and positioning to page elements. In this workflow, we want to handle those two tasks separately because we're using two deliverables to articulate our ideas. The prototype is for layout, and the style guide is for style. This way we can create the layout with input from user experience (UX) designers, and the style with input from art directors, without the two disciplines offering conflicting feedback.

In our CSS, the two concerns can be combined in the same file, but a distinction in class naming will provide better structure to the overall CSS.

We want to hide the off-canvas navigation first, as we did in chapter 4, and make the interface elements visible. To see this in detail, check out index.html and style.css in the 5.8 directory of this chapter's code.

```
.wrapper{
  width:100%;
  position:relative;

  -webkit-transition:all 1.0s ease-in-out;
  -moz-transition:all 1.0s ease-in-out;
  -o-transition:all 1.0s ease-in-out;
  transition:all 1.0s ease-in-out;
}

[...]

#topHeader .left-tray{left:-50%;}
#topHeader .right-tray{right:-50%;}
```

Use CSS transitions to animate the canvas. CSS3 transitions control the animation speed when you change an element property.

Negative positioning to hide the off-canvas elements. We'll use jQuery to add state classes to hide and show these later.

With these pieces in place, we need to add a little jQuery code to make the layout move around.

5.2.3 Animating the off-canvas elements

Now we're going to add classes to the body tag on the page to communicate page states. In figure 5.9 you can see the off-canvas navigation expanded.

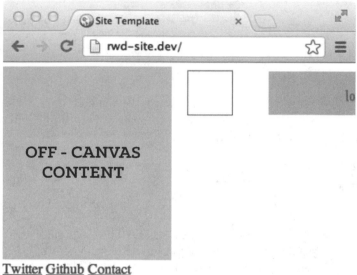

Figure 5.9 The left off-canvas element expanded

In order to implement the off-canvas navigation, we have to toggle between CSS classes that will define the positioning of the wrapper (`.wrapper`). We'll do this with a touch of jQuery. For each of the buttons (`infoTray` and `navTray`), we're going to define a `click` function that will toggle the respective CSS class in the body of the page. By adding this class to the body, we can affect multiple elements on the page simultaneously without having to add multiple classes. This will reflect interface state page-wide:

```
$("#infoTray").click(function(){
  $("body").toggleClass("info-active");
});

$("#navTray").click(function(){
  $("body").toggleClass("nav-active");
});
```

Next, we need some CSS to support our states:

```
.info-active .wrapper{left:50%;}
.nav-active .wrapper{right:50%;}
```

We now have a simple off-canvas design pattern. Because we're focusing on layout styles, it's going to look completely unstyled, but the base is there, and we can start adding design elements. The source code for this is found in the 5.8 directory of the chapter's source code.

With this header in place, let's make this element responsive. We're going to do this for each element, so we can focus on one element at a time while we step through the page width and make each modular element on the page function appropriately.

5.2.4 *Making the element responsive*

In responsive web design, a site is only complete when it will work for a range of site widths (you will want to focus on the widths that are used by the devices that have the largest audiences, because each breakpoint that you customize will required time and resources). We have a nice starting point for our website, but now we need to expand it for wider views, or we'll just have a gigantic mobile website.

ADDING MEDIA QUERIES TO MAKE THE HEADER RESPONSIVE

When you're building a responsive site, you need to use the same HTML elements on the page to create different layouts for different screen sizes. You want to have a single HTML base and very few hidden objects on the pages. You want to avoid the trap of toggling between HTML elements at assigned breakpoints simply because a particular device has a certain viewport. New devices with new resolutions are coming out all the time, so your goal should be to make something fluid that doesn't depend on a few set viewports.

In our example design, our first breakpoint is at about 720 pixels. This is a good breakpoint, because although the elements still seem to work well at this size, there's some open space to play in. At our first breakpoint, we need to consider the amount of space we now have and take advantage of it according to our site's priorities. Because the content on the left is supplemental and the content to the right is site navigation, leading users to different top-level sections of the website, the content to the right takes priority.

Developer insight: tracking viewport with console.log

One thing that makes my life much easier is logging the current viewport width to the browser console. This gives me an absolute number to base my media queries on.

To log the viewport width, call `console.log(document.body.clientWidth);` in JavaScript.

Also, major browser vendors provide developer tools, which makes life easier. For example, if you open the settings in the Chrome developer console, you can dock the tools to the right. The browser will retain its viewport width, minus the size of the inspector tools, so you can preview a mobile site and have a large console at the same time.

What we want to do is open up some of the space on the right to give us room for navigation. To do this, we can move the logo left and then add the site navigation links to the right side of the header. We also need to hide the navigation button on the right, since we won't be using it. The following code does this at a breakpoint for 720 pixels:

```css
@media (min-width: 720px){

  #navTray{display: none;}

  #topHeader .right-tray{
    width:auto;
```

Media query for screens with a min-width of 720 pixels.

Hide the navigation button.

```
      padding:10px;
      right:0;
    }

  #topHeader .logo{
    left:70px;
    margin-left:0;
    }
}
```

With a few minimal tweaks, we've changed the layout of the page completely (see figure 5.10).

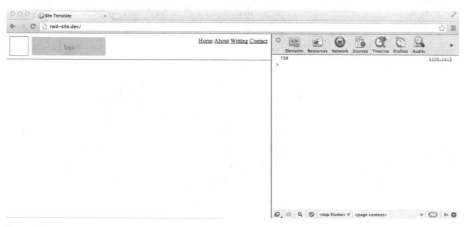

Figure 5.10   Our updated layout

Our breakpoint is a success. Without changing our markup at all, we've adapted our header's layout to fit its new context. But although the right navigation looks great, our left-side elements are now a little off. There's an issue with the left-side navigation in an expanded state. The revised layout is shown in figure 5.11.

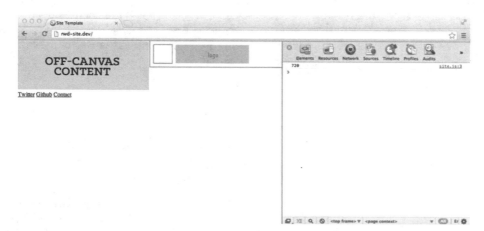

Figure 5.11   Our expanded information panel at the left of the page looks out of place in the larger viewport.

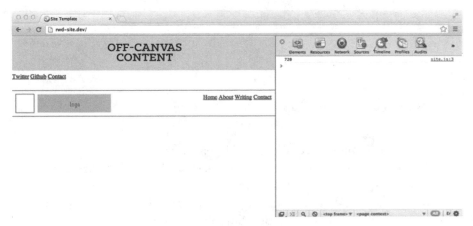

Figure 5.12   Our navigation now drops down from the top.

In this larger context, the content within the off-canvas navigation doesn't seem to justify its screen real estate. Let's change the way this button works, while keeping its core as intact as possible.

The easiest way to do this is to change the CSS, and the most elegant way is not to change how the navigation functions, but to change where the interaction takes place. Instead of hiding the off-canvas elements to the left, let's move them to the top and pull them down into the user's view.

We now have a header in place, with a single breakpoint at 720 pixels, as seen in figure 5.12. From here we can start expanding our page for larger screens. This is going to mean adjusting not just the positioning, but also some of the logic behind our elements.

5.2.5   Expanding into the wider views

When going from tablet to desktop, you can start opening up your layout a bit. You have room to move your elements around a little more. In our case, we want to keep things mostly the same but increase the sizes a little.

The easiest way to set this is with a `max-width` rule on the `.wrapper` class. Because everything within the wrapper is percentage-based, the site should retain its structure. We'll add the following rules to `.wrapper` in the style.css file:

```
max-width: 1024px;
margin:0 auto;
```

Our site will now be framed in a 1,024-pixel-wide wrapper (see figure 5.13). In this breakpoint, you can see the header in its inactive state, with the supplemental material hidden.

Figure 5.13   Our framed site header

Our header now has a lot of empty whitespace, which is okay for the most part. Once we get into designing the page, we'll be glad we have that extra space, because it'll give us more space to expand creatively.

One thing we can do now in the layout phase is increase the size of the logo and decrease the size of the information button, as shown in figure 5.14.

Figure 5.14   A smaller information button

With this new layout, our site functions nicely in a desktop browser. We've created a header module that reacts responsively, both in its interaction and in its layout. We've used few fixed-width elements, instead relying entirely on percentages, giving us a nice degree of fluidity for small and mid-sized screens.

5.3   *Summary*

In this chapter we covered the core fundamentals of building a responsive layout. You learned the basics of using percentages to create a fluid layout. We also discussed how fluid layouts differ from pixel-based layouts, and how they can be changed with media queries.

We touched on the use of `box-sizing` to affect how the box model renders on a page and what its benefits and drawbacks are. We also discussed fluid grid systems, building off-canvas navigation, and hiding content off the page.

We covered a lot of ground in this chapter, but with this bit out of the way, we're ready to proceed and start building responsive layouts. In the following chapters, we'll build on what you've learned and go into more details.

5.4   *Discussion points*

- In creating a responsive web site, what are some of the common pain points in establishing a grid system for a design?

- When building a site, what information do you need to have early on to create a more effective grid system?
- When considering a user's experience on the site, what do you use to communicate interface elements effectively?
- In building a responsive site, what unique elements need specific consideration from designers? If a button is used on both mobile views and desktop views, how does that affect how it's developed?

Adding content modules and typography

This chapter covers

- Adding a content module to the layout
- Building thorough demo content
- Adding web fonts using an external content delivery network

A few years ago, the American public broadcaster NPR began to expand its digital channels. At the time, they had a few iOS and Android apps, as well as a website. To serve content to these channels, they created an API that would feed content to a server; the websites and applications would then request articles from that server and pass them to the users as XML files (see figure 6.1).

By using this API, NPR only had to change the presentation layer to meet the needs of the different platforms, and they could rely on the XML feed for content. As a result, NPR has developed a robust library of applications that listeners can use to consume content in the format and on the device that they prefer.

Although this example is related to developing a suite of applications, the lesson is important. Content is the substance of everything we do online. Layout is the foundation for the content's display, but it's the content itself that the user is visiting for. The formats might change—it might be video, audio, text, or even some sort of experience—but ultimately every visitor is looking for some sort of content.

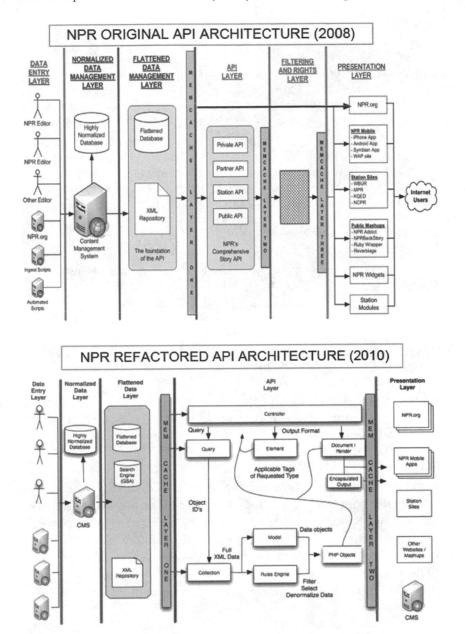

Figure 6.1 NPR's original and new API architectures (from http://blog.programmableweb.com/2011/04/18/what-we-did-wrong-npr-improves-its-api-architecture/)

Designer insight: identifying what the user needs

In the example site we've been developing, the content is pretty clear. We're creating a site to host blog articles. This is a luxury. Sometimes you won't know what the content will be—I've often had clients come to me looking for "a website." They aren't really sure what they want to say or how they want to say it, so the obvious first step for me is to start building a website and then figure out where we need content and start plugging something in. I realize how counterintuitive this process is and how much harm it can do to the creation of a quality experience. Even if a site appears simple, it's crucial to identify why somebody might be there and to build around that purpose.

At one point I was talking with a friend about a site I was building for a nearby restaurant. We talked about what the experience of the site should be and what images and interactions to use. I made the point that 90% of people just want to find a nearby restaurant and look at the menu. "Then that should be your site," he told me. I argued that this would be too simple, that there should be more to it than that. "Why?" he asked me. "You just said that 90% of the visitors just want the menu and the location. Why can't it just be that?"

My friend made a point that changed how I look at the content of the pages I build. If you know what people want, why waste time and money building something nobody will use?

What do users want from our blog site? The site is an outlet for writing and for sharing ideas on web development, so written content is our focus. We want the most recent article front and center when the user visits. A typical post includes an image, a headline, the publication date, and tags.

In this chapter, we'll create a content area in a mobile view. All the techniques in this chapter can be applied to any responsive site you're working on, because almost all sites have and need content.

6.1   Adding a content module

In the first two chapters, we discussed the benefits of designing sites for mobile first. When taking this approach, it's important to identify the necessary components of the site and how their space needs are adjusted as the width of a site increases. Width is a fixed resource in the browser window, as we discussed in the previous chapters. This is one of the most visible driving factors behind the need for responsive websites, and it has the deepest effect on how you curate the content of your site.

Let's get started with the coding of our content module.

Designer insight: space- and content-aware design

I have a close friend who is a talented painter and artist. When she sets up an art exhibit, she always goes to the space where the exhibit is being held so she can choose the right work to display. It's crucial to the work that she curates her exhibits in the

(continued)

context of the space they will occupy. This is similar to the task that we as developers take on in building and designing our sites. Often our role is that of curator, but in order to properly curate our sites, we have to first be aware of the space our content will be displayed in. It involves more than simply making the content of the site bigger or smaller; it involves determining what's important and how it is best consumed.

Each of our content modules is like a piece of art. Each has its unique properties and purposes. The content might be a video, a block of text, an image, or an experience, but more often than not it's a combination of these.

6.1.1 Creating useful placeholder content

In our prototype (figure 1.8), we included a few paragraphs of placeholder text. Now we need to add a set of commonly used HTML elements into our placeholder article so we can start building a typographic base for our written content. You'll want to see how inline elements, such as bolded text, links, and italicized text, as well as block elements, such as unordered lists and headlines within the article, use standard HTML tags.

This typographic base will be the beginning of a typographic standard for our site. Although we don't want to start defining typefaces yet (we'll do that later in this chapter using the typefaces specified in chapter 3's style tile), we'll put the elements in place so we can see how they look as the site expands and the layout changes.

The HTML markup will look something like this (it's included in the 6.1 directory of this chapter's source code):

```
<section role="main">
    <article>
      <figure class="masthead-image">
        <img src="http://placehold.it/400x200" />
      </figure>
      <hgroup>
        <h1>Article Headline Sample - Character count of 47</h1>
        <h2>Article reenforcing sub headline - character count of 56</h2>
      </hgroup>
      <aside class="article-data">
        <time>01/01/2012</time>
        <span class="tag-cloud">
          <a href="#">tag</a>, <a href="#">tag</a>,
          <a href="#">tag</a>
        </span>
      </aside>
      <p>Lorem ipsum dolor sit amet
        <b>inline bold element</b> [...]
        <a href="#">inline text link</a> [...]
        <i>inline italics</i> [...]
        dolore magna aliqua. [...]
      </p>
```

HTML 5 tags provide semantic meaning to the structure of the component; semantic HTML is processed by user agents (such as search spiders or screen readers).

```
    <span>Unordered List:</span>
    <ul>
      <li>List Item</li>
      <li>List Item</li>
      <li>List Item</li>
      <li>List Item</li>
    </ul>
    <p>Lorem ipsum [...] </p>
    <span>Ordered List:</span>
    <ol>
      <li>List Item</li>
      <li>List Item</li>
      <li>List Item</li>
      <li>List Item</li>
    </ol>
    <p>Lorem ipsum [...].</p>
    <p>Lorem ipsum [...] </p>
    <h1>In Article Headline 1</h1>
    <h2>In Article Headline 2</h2>
    <h3>In Article Headline 3</h3>
    <h4>In Article Headline 4</h4>
    <h5>In Article Headline 5</h5>
    <p>Lorem ipsum [...] </p>
    <figure>
      <img src="http://placehold.it/300x300?text=placeholder-image" />
      <figcap>Example caption</figcap>
    </figure>
    <p>Lorem ipsum [...] </p>
    <p>Lorem ipsum [...]</p>
  </article>
</section>
```

HTML 5 tags provide semantic meaning to the structure of the component; semantic HTML is processed by user agents (such as search spiders or screen readers).

This covers all the elements included in the prototype, as well as a good number of base-level typographical elements. There's a lot of base level content here, and I've kept the use of classes to a minimum because, again, we're only looking at the site's core. We want to focus on this core because it gives us a large set of elements that we can anticipate using in our final product.

If we modeled our core around a single blog post, we couldn't possibly anticipate all the content types we'd need as the site grows. For instance, one post might only need some paragraphs and an image, but another might need unordered lists and inline bold elements. When building a core for a site, it's best to anticipate the various use cases early.

Now we have a lot of unstyled markup without any CSS to govern its layout. Without CSS in place, our content is going to look pretty rough. Take a look at the left side of figure 6.2.

As it stands, our page looks pretty raw, which is fine, but some pieces overlap and the layout needs to be put in place. We're going to use CSS to tidy things up, and then we can start making some typographic decisions:

Use **HTML role attribute** because this section is the "main" content of the document. Role has value in accessibility, and it's also useful as a **CSS selector** because it holds a higher specificity value as it uses both attribute (section) and property (role) selector.

```
section[role="main"]{
  padding: 70px 10px 0;
}

figure{width: 100%;}
figure img{width:100%; height:auto;}
```

Add a little padding to the top and sides of the section wrapper. The padding on top offsets the header, which is positioned absolutely and is therefore removed from the DOM order. Elements positioned absolutely are always positioned relative to their parent element and according to assigned top, bottom, left, and right coordinates.

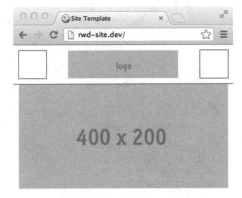

Figure 6.2 Two versions of our content module. On the left, the content module is full and in place. On the right, the content within the module has some subtle changes applied with CSS.

Now that we've put our content in place and the header and content are no longer overlapping, let's apply some rules so we can govern the content's positioning. We're going to apply a light gray background and then add some sizing rules.

To review, our HTML looks like this:

```
<aside class="article-data">
  <time>01/01/2012</time>
  <span class="tag-cloud"><a href="#">tag</a>, <a href="#">tag</a>, <a
    href="#">tag</a></span>
</aside>
```

To position the aside elements, we'll apply style and layout with the following CSS rules:

```
.article-data{
  width:30%;
  padding:5%;
  margin:0 5% 5% 0;
  float: left;
  background:#ccc;
}

.article-data time{
  display: block;
}
```

CSS class rule that floats the element, provides background styling, and defines width, padding, and margin values

CSS rule that defines the display value of all the time HTML elements inside an element with the .article-data CSS class

This produces the layout shown in figure 6.3.

Figure 6.3   Our sidebar in place, with the date and three tags. In the left version, the "article-data" aside is unstyled, and on the right the "article-data" aside has style and float applied to it, giving it the grey box and adjusting the content to the left side of the parent element.

We now have our content module laid out and we're ready to start moving the scale up. This process will be similar to what we did in previous chapters when we adjusted the layout elements for larger screens, or where we adjusted the grid layout, so we won't go through the layout tweaks for bigger viewports. What's important here is how the content—specifically the typography—*looks* in the scaled-up viewports.

6.2   *Typography in responsive design*

Typography is the art of combining typefaces, font sizes, line lengths, white space, word spaces, line breaks, and all other elements that represent visual text. It's an absolutely crucial part of web design, because most of the web's content comes in the form of the written word.

It's difficult for a designer to anticipate exactly what form that written content will take, particularly in a blog, where the content will vary from entry to entry. One of the most common problems occurs when a site is designed to house a finite amount of content. If design takes precedence over function and content, a site can be prone to breaking. For instance, a designer might mock up a headline in a layout based on some placeholder copy. When the design is adjusted for mobile, tablet, and desktop views, the placeholder copy remains the same. If the designer hasn't allowed for variation, such as a headline that's three lines long instead of the two in the mockup, the layout will need to be adjusted. Similarly, if the headline is only one line of text, it may leave a big open space where the design expects more headline to go.

When designing content areas, it's absolutely crucial to keep this problem in mind. One of the ways to combat this is to set a character count for the articles, but this can be cumbersome to maintain. Imagine CMS builds where every text input has a minimum and maximum text length to keep the page consistent. It could take days of work, and in the end the client may find these constraints too limiting.

Because content is always being generated, and therefore is always evolving, producing prototypes and style tiles, then layouts, and finally applying the design is a better route than wedging content into a design. In this section, we'll go over a few ways you can design content for the web and start to establish the visual identity of the site.

6.2.1 Embedding typefaces

In chapter 3 (figure 3.5), we set some typefaces in our style tile: Nunito for body copy and subheads and Lora for headlines. In order to render these fonts on the page, we'll take advantage of Google Fonts (discussed in chapter 2). It's free to use and hosts a wide variety of typefaces. There are other services available that charge for use, but for our purposes we'll stick with Google.

> ### Designer insight: web fonts
>
> Web fonts offer a lot of options for designers and can make a site look great, but they're also easy to abuse. It's easy to use too many fonts, or fonts that aren't available or licensed for web use.

First, you need to find the fonts in Google Fonts. This is as simple as visiting www.google.com/fonts and entering the font name into the search field on the left or browsing for a font that looks good. For this example, search for Nunito.

Once you've found the proper typeface, you need to include style variations (as in figure 6.4). To do so, click the Add to Collection button to add the default *normal*

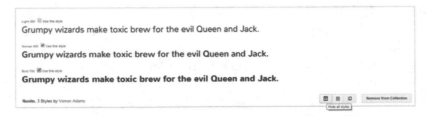

Figure 6.4 Selecting the styles to use. Be careful to only add the styles you need. Browsers do a good job of italicizing text on their own, but I recommend selecting a bold style if it's available, because font weight can render awkwardly in the browser.

variation. To view and select other variations, click the Show All Styles icon and select the variations you want to include. The Normal and Bold styles are included in figure 6.4 (Normal 400 and Bold 700).

Do this again for the Lora typeface and you should have your collection. With Lora, you only need to add the bold style, because you'll only use it for headlines.

Once you're done, click Use and proceed to get the code needed. In this screen you can adjust the typefaces in use to reduce the page burden. A little further down, you'll find the link to include the fonts on your page. It should be included in the head of your HTML document and should look like this:

```
<link href='http://fonts.googleapis.com/css?family=Lora:700|Nunito:400,700'
    rel='stylesheet' type='text/css'>
```

The linked resource will include the three required font faces specified in the `href` link, right after `css?`: `?family=Lora:700|Nunito:400,700`. The numbers after the font names are the font styles. For Lora the request is for the bold 700 style and for Nunito both normal 400 and bold 700 styles. This will be the typographic palette.

Your fonts are now ready to be used on the page. You can call the fonts in your CSS and start setting the typographic core for the site.

Developer insight: CSS file structure

In the code samples, all of the CSS is in a single stylesheet to keep things in one place for your reference. Personally, I like to use separate files for my typographic base and core layout styles.

I also like having all my CSS for the mobile site in a single stylesheet, which is the only stylesheet I serve to mobile devices. This keeps the mobile load time as low as possible.

Ultimately I like to maintain a working base of two or three files, depending on total site size: one file for core layout, type, and mobile CSS, another for mid-sized or tablet browsers (if necessary), and another for desktop browsers. Sometimes a separate tablet file isn't necessary, depending on the variance between mobile and desktop.

6.2.2 Setting a typographic base

Because content is the absolute core of our page, setting the base for the site's typography is a crucial step. In some cases you might find that your core content is video or images, but even in these cases the web requires a lot of written content. Setting the type is like setting the base melody in a symphony. Once you have your melody in place, you can start building upon that. The base may change at times or require some tweaking, but it serves as a nice foundation on which the site can grow.

Let's start by adding the appropriate typefaces to the high-level selectors. Because almost all of the copy will rely on the Nunito typeface, you can set that as the body font with this line of CSS at the top of the stylesheet:

```
body{font-family:'Nunito', arial, sans-serif ;}
```

Now you can override this style on your h1 tags with this code:

```
h1{font-family: 'Lora', 'Times New Roman', serif}
```

Now that you're using the fonts from Google, as seen in figure 6.5, you need to set the sizes. In chapter 1 we discussed using the em instead of pixels for font sizing. Let's put this knowledge to use here.

You want to find an easily readable size for your type—20 pixels is a good starting point. You can set the font-size on the body tag to 20px so you have a base to start with, and you can adjust from there:

```
body{
   font-size: 20px;
   font-family:'Nunito', arial, sans-serif ;
}
```

The h1 tag should contain the biggest font on the page (this could change in different content modules, but bear with me on this one). Remember, when setting em sizes, 1 em is always relative to the parent element's font-size. In this case 1 em is 20 pixels. After some dabbling in the mobile view, I've found 1.75 em to be a nice starting point:

```
h1{
   font-size: 1.75em;
   font-family: 'Lora', 'Times New Roman', serif;
}
```

Article Headline Sample - Character count of 47

Article reenforcing sub headline - character count of 56

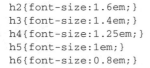

01/01/2012
tag, tag, tag

Lorem ipsum dolor sit amet inline bold element, consectetur adipisicing elit inline text link, sed do *inline italics* eiusmod tempor incididunt ut labore et dolore magna aliqua. Ut enim ad minim veniam, quis nostrud exercitation ullamco laboris nisi ut aliquip ex ea commodo consequat. Duis aute irure dolor in reprehenderit in voluptate velit ess cillum dolore eu fugiat nulla

Figure 6.5   The web fonts in action. As you can see, the site is beginning to take on a little more personality.

From here, you can start balancing out the headers. The header text sizes should get incrementally smaller, ending with an H6, which I like to make smaller than the body copy:

```
h2{font-size:1.6em;}
h3{font-size:1.4em;}
h4{font-size:1.25em;}
h5{font-size:1em;}
h6{font-size:0.8em;}
```

In figure 6.6, we've scaled down our headings, but with only one minor adjustment to the CSS. It's important to keep in mind as you build your site that if you want a smaller headline, you should resist the temptation to scale down the tag using CSS. Instead, try using the proper tag for the size you want.

The process of writing utilitarian CSS also applies to creating classes for modules. Once you have a base, you might find that in another module you want a smaller typeface, such as for some thumbnails at the bottom of the page. You can keep your site styles consistent and change the size of the type contained across multiple objects by applying a class to the shared parent element. As a site evolves between viewports, type that might look great on one screen might be too small or big on another.

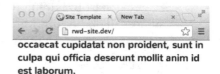

Figure 6.6   The headlines are now easily readable, and they size down nicely.

6.3   Summary

In this chapter we added a content module and filled it with content. We also discussed how to build a base typographic palette and include some sizing and styles. In doing this, we're preparing the canvas for our content.

We started with a simple prototype and a style tile, and now we've got something that's starting to look like a website. With a little more work, we'll have something that looks even more like a well-designed website. In the next chapter, we'll add graphics and apply more of our visual brand to the page.

6.4   Discussion points

- How does building modular CSS affect your build and design processes?
- When considering what typefaces to use for a design, what do you consider?
- If you use Photoshop or any other graphic editing program, does its user interface allow for designing modularly? If so, how?

Part 3

Expanding the design with code

In part 3 we'll dive into the code. Here you're not just going to learn how to use HTML and CSS to build a basic web page. We're going to talk in detail about some of the challenges that are unique to responsive web design.

In chapter 7 we'll discuss adding graphics to a page. This includes ways to use CSS3 to optimize for performance and small screens.

Then, in chapter 8 you'll start learning about progressive enhancement. With progressive enhancement you can create websites so that they function well in a variety of platforms, each with their own limitations and specifications.

Finally, in chapter 9, we'll talk about testing and optimization. Here we'll get into the nitty gritty of optimizing your website for performance on every screen.

Adding graphics in the
browser with CSS

This chapter covers

- Using CSS as a design tool
- Maintaining proportions in a responsive site
- Adding responsive media
- Using icon fonts in your design
- Using SVG in modern sites

It was tempting to title this chapter "Designing in the Browser" because we're now at what might commonly be referred to as a "detail design" phase. We've already designed the site, and we've discussed the user interface, content, visual brand, and identity; everything is ready for us to start crafting a more detailed presentation layer.

In chapter 2 we used Photoshop to create a presentation layer for our site (figure 2.8). This showed designers how to take their typical workflow and apply it to mobile design. In this chapter, we're going to execute a lot of those ideas, but with one huge variation: we're not going to use Photoshop; we'll use Cascading Style Sheets (CSS). With CSS3 you can add gradients, round corners, drop shadows (on text as well as on elements), color models for both RGB colors and alpha transparency, and opacity. In addition to features that enable beautiful design, CSS lets you animate between states, and because it renders natively in the browser, it also looks sharp and vibrant in high-resolution screens, such as Retina displays. This enables you to avoid the messy business of detecting high-resolution displays and serving alternative files to those browsers.

7.1 Using CSS to implement design

Let's look back to our style tile from chapter 3 (shown in figure 7.1) as a guide in making decisions regarding color and visual appearance.

Developer insight: designing in phases

For most developers, designing web pages is a boring and intimidating task. An understanding and respect of web design basics is crucial to success in front-end development, but it's important not to get too hung up trying to perfect a web design yourself. The process described in this book is intended to be highly iterative and collaborative.

In my daily work, I find myself relying on other people for their expertise, and they rely on me for mine. This is the nature of collaboration, and it's important to keep that in mind. Building web sites and applications is more of a team sport today than ever.

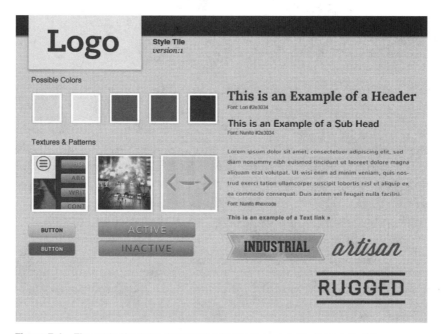

Figure 7.1   The style tile from chapter 3 will serve as a guide for our design.

Using the style tile as a guide, we'll start with the basics and select a color scheme and some patterns or background texture. We'll use small images to create background patterns. With just a little CSS, we can produce the page in figure 7.2. For the CSS involved in creating this page, see the 7.1 directory in this chapter's source code.

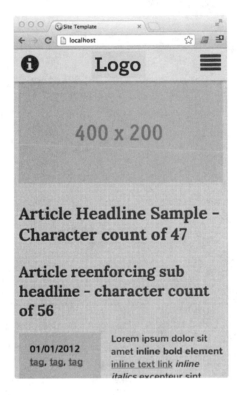

Figure 7.2 The beginnings of a designed page

7.1.1 CSS basics

Most of the CSS is rudimentary, but there are a few things worth pointing out. The first is on line 77:

```
#infoTray, #navTray{
  position:absolute;
  top:0;
  width:50px;
  height:50px;

  background-size: 100% auto;
  background-repeat: no-repeat;
  background-position: center center;
}
```

> The background-size property sets the display rules for the background image's size.

The first property worth mentioning is `background-size`. This property allows you to set the size of a background image. Its syntax is

```
background-size: [x value] [y value];
```

and the values can be sizes in pixel or percentage values, as well as the following three keywords:

- `auto`—Automatically scales the image so its proportions are retained.
- `cover`—Scales the image to entirely cover the size of the related object. Some parts of the image may not be in view in the background area.

- contain—Ensures the image covers as much of the object's area as possible, without distorting the image. All of the image will be in view, but it may not cover all of the background area.

Next there's the box-shadow property. This gives you the ability to add a small shadow to the header, which we'll add alongside a background color to give the header some depth:

```
#topHeader{
  position:absolute;
  top:0;

  width:100%;
  height:50px;

  background:#efebe3;
  box-shadow:0 0 5px #000;
}
```

The box-shadow property is applied to give a small, gradual shadow to the object.

The box shadow property syntax is

```
box-shadow: [x distance] [y distance] [blur] [color];
```

The x, y, and blur values can be set with pixel values, and color can be set with a hex or RGB value, or an RGBA value, which allows better control over shading with its ability to apply alpha transparency.

A major issue you may face is displaying an image with a consistent proportion or aspect ratio. When working in fluid measurements, it can be trying to ensure images retain the proper dimensions and scale. Let's see how CSS can solve the problem.

7.1.2 *Maintaining proportions in a fluid structure*

In a scalable and responsive website, the height and width of images or media elements often need to maintain a relationship. A 3:4 image might need to be displayed at a width of 200 pixels on one device and 400 pixels on another but still maintain the same proportions. One way of doing this with images is by declaring a CSS height of auto, but what about elements that don't have an embedded height value, such as an element with a background image?

There's a trick in CSS to help with this. In our current example (figure 7.2), it's used on the logo. In the mobile screen size, we want the logo to display at a width of 100 pixels, but on larger screens we want the logo to increase in height as well as width. We can use the same technique here that we discussed in section 1.3.3 for adding scalable images.

Figure 7.3 The logo should maintain a consistent relationship between width and height.

To create a consistent relationship between width and height, we'll use an h1 tag to display the logo, as seen in figure 7.3, and use a wrapper to constrain the proportions. The logo shown in the h1 should be able to scale proportionally with the width of the parent element:

```
<div class="logo-wrapper">
    <h1 id="logo">Logo</h1>
</div>
```

Wrap the logo h1 header inside a convenient constraining element.

Then we'll create CSS rules for both the wrapper and the logo header:

```
.logo-wrapper{
  position:relative;
  width:100px;
  left:50%;
}

#logo{
  position:absolute;
  overflow:hidden;
  width:100%;
  height:0px;
  padding-bottom:44%;
  font-size:0px;
  background: url(/images/logo.png) no-repeat;
  background-size:cover;
}
```

Positioning is the key to making this trick work. Relative positioning is essentially the default positioning, but the child's positioning (#logo) is given in relation to its parent.

The percentage-based padding of an element is always relative to the width of its parent, which is why it can be used to draw a relationship between width and height.

First, we set the parent to the desired width. In this case we want it set to 100 pixels, but we could just as easily use an em or a percentage value. We also need to set the positioning to relative. This is important because we need to set an absolute position for the child element in order to maintain the sizing.

Percentage-based height is always relative to an ancestor with an explicit height, but percentage-based padding is always consistent (top and bottom, left and right), and always relative to the parent element. Therefore, padding-bottom is relative to the width of a parent element. We can exploit this to our advantage in responsive websites.

Another place this CSS trick comes in handy is with video. Videos almost always require a set aspect ratio (see figure 7.4 and the 7.2 directory in the chapter's source code).

Figure 7.4 A responsive video in place

An aspect ratio is easily applied to a video by wrapping the video in a container `div` (instead of the usual `iframe` HTML element) that will define the available area for the video:

```
<div class="video-wrapper">
  <iframe src="http://www.youtube.com/embed/9bZkp7q19f0" frameborder="0"
    allowfullscreen></iframe>
</div>

.video-wrapper{
    position: relative;
    padding-bottom: 56.25%;
    height: 0;
    overflow: hidden;
}

.video-wrapper iframe{
    position: absolute;
    top: 0;
    left: 0;
    width: 100%;
    height: 100%;
}
```

A padding-bottom sets the wrapper's aspect ratio because percentage-based padding is set against the DOM object's width (instead of the parent element's height, as a height percentage is).

overflow:hidden ensures the object size depends on what's drawn with padding-bottom.

By setting the height to zero, we rely on padding-bottom to size the object on the page.

Set absolute positioning to keep the iframe in place. Top and left put the iframe in the corner, and the width ensures the video fills the parent object completely.

Using the preceding HTML and CSS, the video will scale nicely between views. The video `iframe` will scale fully from right to left and maintain a proper aspect ratio, as you can see at the bottom of figure 7.5.

Now let's look at some ways we can add user interface graphics to the page.

7.2   Using icon fonts in your design

With CSS3 you can load custom typefaces into your designs, as we discussed in chapter 6. This has obvious advantages for creating unique designs in the browser, but it can also be exploited to create beautiful user interfaces using icon fonts. An icon font is a custom typeface that's based on scalable vectors (SVG). With an icon font, you can easily change the color, size, and everything else you can do with any typeface.

7.2.1   User interface sprites

Typically, user interface controls for websites are implemented by creating a CSS sprite, which is a collection of images combined in a single image (see figure 7.6), and displaying the parts of the image in that

Figure 7.5   The aspect ratio difference between a video using just the `iframe` tag (top) and using the container `div` (bottom).

sprite as they're needed. A single image is used as the background for an element, and the portion displayed is aligned by using the `background-position` CSS property.

This has traditionally been an effective method, but in a responsive website it needs to be slightly more nuanced. High-resolution displays will display a fuzzier image than normal displays, and in smaller screens you might want to use smaller or larger buttons, which would require new sprites for various breakpoints.

The best way around this is to use an icon font face instead of a sprite. Because it's a custom typeface, the icons are vector-based as opposed to the raster-based

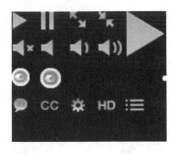

Figure 7.6   An example of a commonly used image sprite, this one from Videojs.com

images in a typical PNG sprite, and you can manipulate each icon as you would any other font family. The font face also scales elegantly for various size requirements.

Designer insight: vector images vs. rasterized images

The difference between vector images and rasterized images is important in responsive web design due to the need to accommodate various pixel densities. One way to describe the difference is that Photoshop produces rasterized images and Illustrator produces vector images.

Rasterized images contain pixel data and create an image by assigning each pixel a color. Displaying such an image becomes challenging when pixel sizes are revised by changing requirements. An image that's created at 100 pixels wide looks "pixelated" when it's stretched to 200 pixels wide.

Vector images, on the other hand, are created by setting points and mathematically drawing lines and curves between them. Because there is no "pixel" data being communicated, the vector images can scale fluidly. Fonts are, by default, vector-based images, but there are other ways of creating vector art for use on the web, most notably the SVG format, which we'll discuss in section 7.3.

7.2.2   *Font-based user-interface graphics*

In our example site, we'll use an open source font for user interface icons called Font Awesome. The font of icons is free to use and is also available through a public content delivery network (CDN), such as the Google CDN we used earlier for our custom typefaces. The CDN I'm using for Font Awesome is cddjs.com.[1]

---

[1]   Font Awesome is a free and open source font: http://fontawesome.io/.

Figure 7.7 shows some of the icons available on Font Awesome.

Figure 7.7   A small example of icons available in Font Awesome

In figure 7.8 I've used Font Awesome to create the information icon and the four-bar navigation icon.

Figure 7.8   Our site's UI, at the top of the page, is generated using a typeface instead of images.

To use this font, you have to add a link reference to the font file. This is similar to the process of linking a font from Google Fonts, as we did in chapter 6. The first thing you do is import the CSS library into your page:

```
<link rel="stylesheet" href="http://cdnjs.cloudflare.com/ajax/libs/font-
    awesome/4.0.3/css/font-awesome.min.css" type="text/css" charset="utf-8">
```

After that, you can add a few classes to the buttons:

```
<span id="infoTrayBtn" class="icon-info-sign btn">
  <i class="fa fa-info"></i>
</span>
<div class="logo-wrapper">
    <h1 id="logo">Logo</h1>
</div>
<span id="navTrayBtn" class="icon-align-justify btn">
  <i class="fa fa-bars"></i>
</span>
```

Add the class fa to the HTML element that will serve as the container for the font, and then add the class of the specific icon that you want, such as fa-info for the information font icon.

NOTE Open source development releases new versions quickly. At the time this was written, the latest version of Font Awesome was 4.0.3.

Then use the `btn` class to style the buttons in the same way you'd style any other type on the page:

```
.btn{
    font-size:2.2em;
    color:#2e3034;
    text-align:center;
}
```

In just a minute or two, you've created a simple user interface that will scale nicely and look gorgeous on high-resolution displays, mostly thanks to the fact that font faces are rendered on the page using Scalable Vector Graphics (SVG). In the case of Font Awesome, these vector graphics come in the form of font files in order to work across different browsers. The vectors themselves are the same, but they're implemented by hacking CSS3's font-face properties for ease of embedding.

What if you wanted to leverage the advantages of SVG outside of generic icon fonts, such as for an image on a page? SVG can currently be used in place of traditional background image formats in most browsers and can offer the same high-quality graphics to present your custom design.

7.3 *Using Scalable Vector Graphics*

Scalable Vector Graphics (SVG) is an XML-based image format that has been an open standard since 1999. The file format has only recently been accessible in modern browsers, but it came in at the perfect time.

SVG gives designers the opportunity to create images that remain sharp and beautiful at any scale and in any display. They can be zoomed in on and retain their crispness, or scaled down and retain their detail. Take a look at figures 7.9 and 7.10.

Figure 7.9 This star was created with a raster-based imaging program and is zoomed in to 400% original size.

Figure 7.10   This is the same star created in a vector-based imaging program, also shown zoomed in to 400%.

An SVG file can be created in Illustrator, Photoshop, or a myriad of other programs— I use an application called Sketch (www.bohemiancoding.com/sketch/). Once you've created your graphics, you can save the files as SVG for use on your page.

> **NOTE**   Any vectors created in Photoshop will have to be exported to Illustrator because Photoshop lacks the ability to save SVG files.

Another great feature of the SVG format is that you can edit it with any text editor. With drawing software like Illustrator you can open and edit an SVG and save it without having to export it every time, meaning that designers can make changes to graphics on a page quickly and easily without having to update any CSS.

7.3.1   Adding an SVG image to a page

An SVG image can be added to a web page in one of two ways: as an object HTML element or as a CSS background image. An object is displayed on the page itself, whereas a CSS background image is applied as the style of an HTML object tag. This is a minor, but important, distinction.

Displaying figure 7.8's SVG star on the page is as simple as linking to the source file on the page. In the HTML file, simply add an `<object>` tag and a few attributes, and the image shows up in the browser (figure 7.11).

Figure 7.11   The SVG image on the page

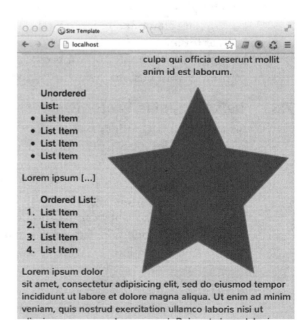

Figure 7.12   The star scaled down

When using an `object` tag to embed an SVG image, you use the `data` attribute to assign the SVG file. This will display the SVG within the `object` tag:

```
<object type="image/svg+xml"
        width="400" height="400" style="float:right"
        data="images/star.svg">
</object>
```

As you can see in figure 7.11, the image retains transparency much like a PNG file and is scaled up to 400 x 400 pixels, as specified in the `object` tag. You can see this transparency in how the page background is visible behind the image of the star. In image formats that don't retain alpha transparency, an image is rendered with a white background. If you wanted to scale this image down, you could change the `width` and `height` values, and the image would still look beautiful (see figure 7.12). See the example code in the 7.3 directory.

The SVG image can be scaled using the `width` and `height` attributes:

```
<object type="image/svg+xml"
        width="100" height="100" style="float:right"
        data="images/star.svg">
</object>
```

It can also be scaled with CSS:

```
<object type="image/svg+xml" class="star"
        data="images/star.svg">
        </object>
```

Note that the `object` tag now has a CSS class `star` that defines the same styles as the `style`, `width`, and `height` properties in the previous example:

```
.star {
    float: right;
    width: 100px;
    height: 100px;
        }
```

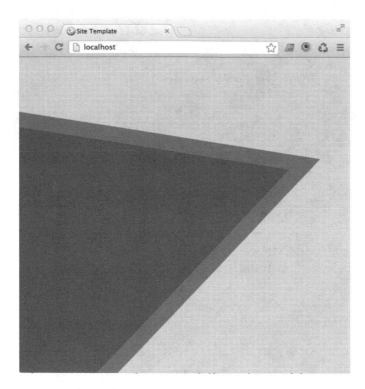

Figure 7.13   An intensely zoomed-in SVG star

Both code samples produce the same result.

   While scaling the image down is helpful, it's not nearly as impressive as when you scale the image up, as shown in figure 7.13. Now the image is scaled to a ridiculous 4,000 x 4,000 size and still looks wonderful.

   Here, I've increased the size of the SVG using the width and height attributes:

```
<object type="image/svg+xml"
        width="4000" height="4000" style="float:right"
        data="images/star.svg">
</object>
```

The file hasn't changed, so the file size is the same—the user isn't burdened with downloading a bigger file to get the bigger image.

7.3.2   *Implementing SVG with CSS*

Being able to add an SVG image to a document is helpful, but using SVG images in CSS can be much more useful at times, such as when you want the image to scale with an object on the page. SVG should be the graphic format of choice when designing a user interface because of its crisp appearance and scalability. This scaling is most easily done in CSS.

   As an example, let's replace our logo with an SVG version. First, you need to create an SVG file using Sketch or some other vector-editing program and export it into the images folder. All you have to do next is replace the PNG in your CSS with an SVG file. The source code for this example is in the 7.4 directory:

```
#logo {
  position:absolute;
  overflow:hidden;
  width:100%;
  height:0px;
  padding-bottom:53%;
  font-size:0px;
  background-image: url(/images/logo.svg);
  background-size:cover;
}
```

The background-image property will load the SVG file that contains the data to generate the graphic (figure 7.14).

What we get is shown in figure 7.14.

You could use a small logo for this site, but in larger views you might want the full size of the logo. This can be done simply by using `background-size`:

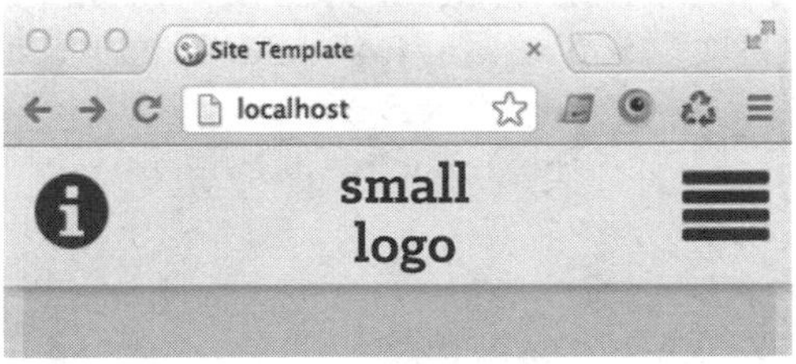

```
#logo {
  position: absolute;
  overflow: hidden;
  width: 131px;
  height: 0px;
  padding-bottom: 53%;
  font-size: 0px;
  background-image: url(/images/logo.svg);
  background-size: 242px auto;
}
```

Figure 7.14 Our logo is now an SVG file.

This scales the logo without compromising image quality by adjusting the size of the background image without affecting the size of the object itself. Even though the object is 131 px wide, its background image is set to 242 px wide, leaving 111 px difference, which is unseen, because it extends outside of the DOM object.

This might be how you'd want to handle a sprite with SVG. The `background-size` setting changes the scale at which the image is rendered without affecting the object the image is rendered within. The `background-size` property is not to be confused with `background-position`, which dictates an image's placement within a DOM object.

7.3.3   *Limitations of the SVG format*

Working with new technology always has its consequences, and the SVG format is no different. Although it gives designers and developers a much higher degree of quality, it comes at a cost, and you need some foresight to overcome the limitations.

FILE SIZE

The most obvious consequence is file size. The file for the star example comes in at just a handful of bytes, but the logo is 70 KB, which is pretty large considering its PNG equivalent is only 9 KB. This issue can be overcome with server-side gzip compression, but it's still important to keep track of how many files are being loaded and how large they are.

SINGLE-COLOR FILES

Another complication is that SVG only works well with illustrations, where color boundaries remain simple. You can apply color and gradients to shapes, but complex images come at an expense in file size. This is why SVG is most useful for user interface elements or site iconography such as Font Awesome, where all the icons are rendered using a single color.

THE SERVER

You also need to make sure that your server will serve SVG files. If you're using an Apache web server, this is as simple as adding a few lines to the server's .htaccess file. If you're not, it should be easy to find an equivalent configuration that will work with your web server configuration.

For Apache, just open your .htaccess file, and add the following two lines at the beginning:

```
AddType image/svg+xml svg
AddType image/svg+xml svgz
```

These lines are the MIME types that ensure your server is configured to read and serve the SVG file format.

BROWSER SUPPORT

The other issue, and probably the most problematic, is browser support. SVG is supported by all modern browsers except Internet Explorer. This can be troublesome, but it's easily solved by creating a PNG file as a fallback when exporting your SVG file:

```
#logo{
    background-image: url(../images/logo.png) no-repeat;
    background-image: url(../images/logo.svg);
}
```

> **If the browser supports SVG, the second declaration of background-image will be used; otherwise it will use the first declaration's PNG version.**

Instead of simply serving the fallback through the typical browser detection, I recommend using feature detection to accomplish this. In the next chapter, we'll discuss feature detection.

7.4 *Summary*

In this chapter we discussed using modern techniques such as font faces and SVG to create and implement beautiful responsive websites.

We talked about creating scalable background images and videos. Using these techniques, images and video elements can scale fluidly in a responsive environment.

We also discussed using icon-based font families to create buttons and UI elements. By using an icon font, you can scale up beautiful, vector-based graphics using CSS.

Finally, we looked at the benefits and implementation of Scalable Vector Graphics (SVG). We discussed the features of SVG images and how to display them on a page and use them in CSS. We also covered the inherent limitations that come with this progressive format.

In the next chapter, we'll discuss ways to overcome some of the cross-browser issues that arise when using modern CSS. We'll discuss Modernizr, a JavaScript library that resolves this issue by basing CSS on feature detection as opposed to assumptions based on browser detection.

7.5 Discussion points

- When it comes to adding graphics to a prototype, how can designers and developers collaborate to achieve a beautiful product?
- What are some of the opportunities that designing in the browser opens up for you?
- What flexibility and benefits do you see to using SVG in your designs? What limitations does it present?

Progressive enhancement and obsolescence control with Modernizr

This chapter covers

- Introducing responsive experiences
- Introducing progressive enhancement
- Diving deeper with Modernizr
- Using Modernizr to progressively enhance an element

So far we've talked about developing a website by starting with prototypes, then moving on to style tiles and content, and finally building the site. The final part of building a responsive site is to use a technique called *progressive enhancement*, enhancing a simple site into one that's more technologically advanced.

The introduction of touch interfaces and small screen devices has been interesting, and they can be fun to design and develop for, but that's merely the tip of the responsive iceberg. Although many users have access to the most modern mobile phones and tablets, building a responsive website also means supporting older, less capable hardware and making content accessible to sight-impaired users.

To achieve this, you first need a workflow that enables you to tend to the needs of all your users. We've talked about designing and developing for mobile first and building up from there, but let's take that further. What if instead of throwing HTML, JavaScript, and CSS at a browser until you get what you want, you build from a basic foundational site and work your way up? Let's see what happens.

8.1 Technical obsolescence

Over time, every website becomes obsolete, and this is especially true in responsive web design. Several techniques have been introduced to deal with this problem, and we'll cover two of them in this chapter: progressive enhancement and graceful degradation.

We'll discuss some of the major points in these two methodologies in order to understand some of the best practices for resolving issues around obsolescence and cross-browser compatibility. Once we've established these two methodologies, we'll discuss how to use Modernizr to achieve a cross-browser-compatible website.

8.1.1 Progressive enhancement

Progressive enhancement is a technique for enhancing a simple site into something that's more technologically advanced, as diagrammed in figure 8.1. This process is a counterpoint to mobile-first design. Mobile-first design deals directly with form, whereas progressive enhancement deals with function. In a progressive enhancement methodology, you start small and gradually make your site more complex by, for example, adding animations or HTML5 and CSS3 features.

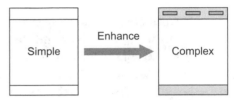

Figure 8.1   This is a simple diagram of the progressive enhancement workflow. You begin with a simple, accessible site and enhance it into a more complex website with modern design features.

When dealing with the function of a site, you first need a model for figuring out how to enhance the site. So far we've discussed using media queries for adjusting the site's layout, but let's see how we can take this mobile-first concept a step further using progressive enhancement to create a responsive experience.

SENSORS, SYSTEMS, AND ACTUATORS

As Mark Boulton described in a blog post titled "A Responsive Experience" (www.markboulton.co.uk/journal/a-responsive-experience), responsive experiences are achieved by using three conceptual components together—sensors, systems, and actuators:

- *Sensors* are components that sense the environment. In the context of responsive web design, the sensor is the browser, which provides valuable information about the user and their current capabilities.
- *Systems* are the responses to the information provided by the sensor. In previous chapters we've discussed media queries, which are a type of system. We could also use JavaScript to build systems that handle events and provide information such as the user's time or geographic location.

- *Actuators* are the responses to the systems' instructions. This could be CSS applied within a media query or a JavaScript plugin that applies page improvements based on the user's capabilities. In previous chapters, our actuators have been the enhancements or adjustments we've made for larger viewports.

So far we've used the browser as a sensor and based our systems on one piece of feedback (viewport width), adjusting accordingly, but there's more to building responsive websites than just responding to width. Width is just the first and simplest way to understand the differences between mobile, tablet, and desktop site versions.

In addition to using media queries to sense the viewport dimensions of a site, there's also a base-level sensor you can use, and that's the lack of JavaScript. The overwhelming majority of web traffic uses JavaScript to render web pages, but with that being said, checking whether or not JavaScript is enabled should be the first sensor you use when progressively enhancing a site. Every site you build should be able to be navigated, to some degree, without JavaScript enabled.

ENHANCING FOR BROWSER VERSIONS

Historically, in front-end development, developers would adjust a site to fit the constraints of the layout engine being used by a particular browser. There were only three browsers in 2003: Netscape, Internet Explorer, and Opera. By 2005, Firefox, Safari, and the first mobile browser, Opera Mini, were released; Chrome was released in 2008.

Currently there are five major browsers, each with its own mobile version. Across that array of browsers, there are also older versions that users haven't upgraded. In the same way that creating multiple layouts for multiple screen sizes eventually becomes a zero sum game, so does building multiple front ends for multiple browsers and browser versions.

We've talked a lot about how to build a site for new, cutting-edge mobile browsers. We're using responsive web design to accommodate these browsers, but it's important not to do so at the expense of older browsers.

Progressive enhancement is one strategy for coping with browsers that don't support up-to-date features. As we've discussed in this book, there's always a temptation to build for the most up-to-date features available, but in a responsive web, design is contextual. The design must be appropriate for the frame that it's being viewed through. Responsive web design has become popular because it resolves the most obvious changing context—the available screen real estate—but the context of a browser runs much deeper than its viewport size.

In the previous chapter we discussed using SVG images in a site's design. SVG is a great solution for high-resolution displays, but what about support in older browsers? It's not supported in IE8 or lower, so you'd have to build in a fallback if you supported that browser. You could identify the browser and serve alternative styles to that browser, but then you'd have to serve those same alternative styles for every browser that doesn't support SVG. Therefore, according to progressive enhancement, you should start the build process with a graphic that's supported by the lowest common denominator, like a PNG. This approach will delay the addition of more modern features for modern browsers in favor of basic functions that are supported by older browsers and devices.

> ### Designer insight: progressive enhancement in design
>
> Progressive enhancement is implemented in development, but it's important to consider ways to support these features during the design process. When progressive enhancement is possible during the design process, it might require a module on a site to be completely replaced with another module that accomplishes the same task. Be ready to provide design starting with a simple layout and progressing into rich and beautiful interfaces.

FEATURE DETECTION VIA USER AGENTS

Traditionally, feature detection has been accomplished by detecting the browser's user agent. This is done through JavaScript, using the navigator object. The navigator object dates back to the Netscape days and used to be a developer's best tool in providing cross-browser compatibility. In the context of sensors and detecting user information in order to resolve a cross-browser issue, user agents were at one time the most meaningful and widely used sensor.

If you have Chrome, Firefox, or Safari available, try opening your browser's web inspector by right-clicking on a page and selecting Inspect Element. After you've opened the web inspector, click on Console, and after the caret, type navigator.userAgent and press Enter. This will return your current browser's user-agent, which is a string of text used to identify the browser in use. For example, I'm using Google Chrome, which returns the following:

```
"Mozilla/5.0 (Macintosh; Intel Mac OS X 10_8_2) AppleWebKit/537.35 (KHTML,
    like Gecko) Chrome/27.0.1443.2 Safari/537.35"
```

In a lot of ways, the navigator object is one of the best sensors we have available to inform our system about what the user is capable of, but it's not very future-friendly. It bases your site's actuators on assumptions about what the browser does and doesn't support. It's also unreliable because it can be configured by the user in order to access sites that the browser might not be able to support.

> ### Developer insight: the navigator object
>
> Although navigator can't reliably be used to make assumptions about the user's feature support, it can be an incredibly handy sensor. In addition to detecting the user agent, it can be used to detect geolocation, whether cookies are enabled, and even where the user is in the world. If your console is still open, try inputting this:
>
> ```
> navigator.geolocation.getCurrentPosition(function(position) {
>   console.log(position.coords.latitude, position.coords.longitude);
> });
> ```

(continued)

The browser should prompt for permission to use your location. If you allow it, it should return two values indicating latitude and longitude. Copy the values into a Google search, and you can see in Google Maps the location your user agent is broadcasting. This can be used as an additional sensor, which you can use to create a richer responsive experience.

For example, on my personal blog I might want to detect whether a visitor is from New York, and if so say something like, "Hey, you're reading my blog, you must be a pretty cool person. I see you're near me, could I take you out for a beer and chat about how to make my site better serve you?" I could potentially use the navigator's geolocation feature to send an alert to such a user, encouraging them to contact me directly.

Detecting user agents is the traditional method of applying progressive enhancement. Developers would know that a certain feature was unavailable to a particular browser and build to that limited specification. An enhancement could be added for a specific browser using its user agent. This was a manageable workflow historically, but now it's unrealistic. There are too many browsers to keep track of, and new operating systems and browser versions are being added daily. Fortunately, there are other methods of resolving cross-browser limitations.

LIMITATIONS OF PROGRESSIVE ENHANCEMENT

In progressive enhancement, you might find yourself having to initially support a minimum system that represents a small percentage of your user base. Say, for instance, that you have a minimum supported browser of IE8—that browser might only represent 5% of your site's traffic, so initial development cycles are spent building support for a product that represents a small subset of actual site traffic.

Meanwhile, if you also decide to work in a mobile-first capacity, you could end up building a site for a mobile device with the features supported in IE8, all to accommodate the limitations of 5% of your site's traffic.

There's another way of dealing with technical obsolescence, through a process known as graceful degradation. This takes the opposite approach to progressive enhancement and involves building a site, and building in a failsafe for each potential failure.

8.1.2 *Graceful degradation*

With graceful degradation, the development of a site includes fallbacks for site failures. This means you might build a site that uses HTML5 video, and if the HTML5 video fails, you use a Flash plug-in to add video support to the browser and play the video.

Unlike progressive enhancement, graceful degradation starts at the most advanced point and falls back to alternatives if browser support fails. This can be an exhausting part of developing a web site. In the quality-control phase of a project, a lot of cross-browser-related bugs find their way to the surface, and developers are forced to react quickly to implement a fallback to fix them.

Providing fallbacks for every module in a page isn't likely to be necessary, or even possible. Fortunately, HTML is backwards-compatible, meaning that HTML5 can work with older browsers using something called a *polyfill*. As Google developer evangelist Paul Irish explains it, a polyfill is a piece of code "that mimics a future API, providing fallback functionality to older browsers" (http://www.paulirish.com/i/7570.png).

HTML5Shiv is an example of a polyfill. It's a piece of code (JavaScript) that mimics a new API (tags introduced in the HTML5 specification, like `<header>` or `<section>`), in order to provide functionality to browsers that don't support the HTML5 specification.

Even with a polyfill in place, some things simply will not work in older browsers. A polyfill is not a major bullet that's going to force browsers to work; it's a piece of code that adds a degree of support for newer features to older browsers.

So when should you use a polyfill? They can be expensive in terms of bandwidth, and loading a lot of polyfills for the few browsers that need them is pretty excessive. You wouldn't want to unnecessarily serve a fallback asset to all mobile browsers simply to give support to some older browsers.

Designer insight: cross-browser perfection

Does every site need to look identical in every browser? I don't think so. If you compare an application on iPhone, Android, Windows, and OS X, does it have to look the same? Of course not; they're completely different platforms, and some common interaction patterns are not going to work as easily across operating systems.

In the youth of the web, developers were expected to make things look uniform in cross-browser environments, but it has become more difficult to maintain uniformity as the internet has diversified. If you want to use WebGL on a project, you can kiss your uniformity goodbye completely. Embracing the fluidity of the web is the whole point of the responsive movement.

If graceful degradation forces you to load too many assets, and progressive enhancement limits your ability to take advantage of new technologies, is there a solution somewhere in the middle? Wouldn't it be easier if you could write one style that would be used against every browser that didn't support SVG? That way you wouldn't have to keep up with every browser's feature set or be surprised when a user reports a bug about an older version of a browser you didn't think anyone used anymore. You could just set the fallback once and forget about it. This is where Modernizr comes in handy.

What if, instead of supporting browsers, we supported features? Then we could create fallbacks for particular features, and browsers that don't support that feature would universally be served the fallback. This is exactly what Modernizr was created for.

8.2   *What is Modernizr?*

Modernizr is a JavaScript library used to detect features in the browser. It's loaded in the head of your page and runs during page load. Adding it to your site is as simple as adding any other JavaScript library, such as jQuery, but once added, Modernizer gives you an incredible amount of control in rendering your page and ensuring that every user is served a quality experience.

When the library is loaded, Modernizr runs a series of checks against the user's browser to determine what features the browser supports, and it creates a JavaScript object that you can test against. Modernizr doesn't create support for these features; it simply gives you a way to provide fallback support for modern features.

Modernizr also applies a set of classes to the html tag, giving you the ability to modify the page's CSS using the generated CSS classes. With these CSS classes, you can use CSS systems to build actuators that will adjust your pages by providing the progressive enhancements available for a page.

Unlike the user agent, Modernizr detects features directly by running a series of JavaScript tests that return Boolean (true or false) values. This dictates the classes that are set on the html tag, and it gives you the ability to use JavaScript to check whether a feature is available. This is done by Modernizr out of the box.

What makes Modernizr unique? Primarily, Modernizr stands alone in that it does something no other library does. HTML5Shiv allows older browsers to recognize and apply style to HTML5 elements, but that's it—HTML5Shiv simply makes HTML5 objects accessible to CSS and JavaScript. Modernizr also does this, but it has the added bonus of feature detection.

HTML5Shiv, in conjunction with browser sniffing, can provide adequate graceful degradation. But it limits the support for a site to specifically identified supported browsers. Any good quality assurance practice should account for a specified amount of browser support, but Modernizr reduces the risk in specifically required HTML5 features.

HTML5Shiv will validate an HTML5 tag like <video>, but what it doesn't do is make an HTML5 video play in an older browser. Although the tag itself can be styled and validated, the source video still won't play in an older browser. Modernizr allows you to not only make this <video> tag valid, but also to offer alternative functionality in the event that the browser doesn't support the feature. In the case of video, you can use Modernizr to fall back to a Flash video player if HTML5 video isn't supported.

There are some cases where Modernizr might not be the right fit. In some cases, you might find Modernizr to be overkill. For instance, if you have a simple site, it might be wise to use the smaller HTML5Shiv to add HTML5 tag support, and then provide a browser-specific CSS file for older versions of Internet Explorer.

Modernizr also blocks page rendering because it needs to append test classes to the HTML classes prior to rendering the visible page. Because it blocks page rendering until the page loads, there can be interference with other JavaScript events, specifically when using libraries like Backbone. These interferences are rare, but they're worth being aware of. In most cases, blocking page rendering will be unnoticeable by the user, but it's a trade-off with Modernizr that's worth being aware of.

8.2.1   *Installing Modernizr*

Installing Modernizr is as simple as linking to the JavaScript library in the head of your page. The only complicated part is creating the version that you need. Modernizr is available for download through its website (http://modernizr.com/) in two versions: the development version and the production version.

As mentioned, Modernizr's relationship to page rendering is essential to its utility. This is why, unlike most scripts, Modernizr should be loaded in the head tag. It's common practice to place script tags at the end of the page body, but Modernizr recommends placing it in the head because the HTML5Shiv that's included must execute before the body, and if you use CSS classes in Modernizr, there's a chance of there being a flash of unstyled content.

The development version is a full 42 KB uncompressed file. This version is great if you're well versed in JavaScript and want to make some tweaks to the tests it performs. Because it's uncompressed, it's easy to read and augment, but it's best left to developers with a firm understanding of JavaScript.

If you're not completely adept at JavaScript, or you'd like to quickly build a customized version of Modernizr, you want the production version of the library. The production version's building tool on the site gives you the ability to create a version with only the tests you require.

This comes in handy when you know you only need a certain set of tests. For instance, your site might not take advantage of CSS box shadows, but it might need to support CSS gradients. Using the build tool, you can include the tests you need and exclude the ones you don't, keeping the source code trim and your users' total load time down.

For our example, I'll work with the development version. I find that when I'm building a site, it's best to work with the full version, and then once I know what features I'll use in the site, I trim the version down.

Installing Modernizr is as simple as linking to the source JavaScript file:

```
<script src="/js/modernizr.js" type="text/javascript"></script>
```

After linking, you can add a class of `"no-js"` to the html tag on the page, like this:

```
<html class="no-js">
```

You're ready to go. Note that if JavaScript is supported and enabled, the `no-js` class is removed by Modernizr and replaced with the test classes, a screenshot of which can be seen in figure 8.2. This way, you can add CSS for pages with JavaScript disabled.

```
<!DOCTYPE html>
▼<html class=" js flexbox flexboxlegacy canvas canvastext webgl no-touch
geolocation postmessage websqldatabase indexeddb hashchange history draganddrop
websockets rgba hsla multiplebgs backgroundsize borderimage borderradius
boxshadow textshadow opacity cssanimations csscolumns cssgradients cssreflections
csstransforms csstransforms3d csstransitions fontface generatedcontent video
audio localstorage sessionstorage webworkers applicationcache svg inlinesvg smil
svgclippaths">
```

Figure 8.2   The rendered `html` tag on a page that has the Modernizr CSS classes applied

In total, Modernizr comes with over 40 built-in tests for HTML5, CSS3, and other features. Table 8.1 offers a short rundown of the key tests, taken directly from the Modernizr documentation.

Table 8.1   Built-in tests in Modernizr

Test type	Feature	Modernizr JS object property/CSS classname
CSS tests	@font-face	fontface
	background-size	backgroundsize
	border-image	borderimage
	border-radius	borderradius
	box-shadow	boxshadow
	Flexible Box Model	flexbox
	hsla()	hsla
	Multiple backgrounds	multiplebgs
	opacity	opacity
	rgba()	rgba
	text-shadow	textshadow
	CSS columns	csscolumns
	Generated content	generatedcontent
	CSS gradients	cssgradients
	CSS reflections	cssreflections
	CSS 2D transforms	csstransforms
	CSS 3D transforms	csstransforms3d
	CSS transitions	csstransitions
HTML tests	applicationCache	applicationcache
	Canvas	canvas
	Canvas text	canvastext
	Drag and drop	draganddrop
	hashchange event	hashchange
	History management	history
	HTML5 audio	audio
	HTML5 video	video
	IndexedDB	indexeddb
	localStorage	localstorage
	sessionStorage	sessionstorage
	Web sockets	websockets
	Web SQL database	websqldatabase
	Web workers	webworkers

As you can see, Modernizr covers a lot of ground. We'll go over the basics so you know how to implement feature detection for CSS features and how to access the JavaScript object property for a test.

8.2.2 Using Modernizr for cross-browser CSS

With Modernizr installed, you have everything in place to start making some progressive enhancements. We'll start with a raw sample site:

```
<!doctype html>
<html class="no-js" lang="en">
  <head>
    <meta charset="utf-8">
      <script type="text/javascript" src="//cdnjs.cloudflare.com/ajax/libs/
      modernizr/2.6.2/modernizr.min.js"></script>
  </head>
  <body>

  </body>
</html>
```

In the last chapter we used SVG graphics, so let's use a small test to detect whether or not a browser is capable of supporting SVG. For the sake of simplicity, we'll just add two span tags to the page to detect support:

```
<!doctype html>
<html class="no-js" lang="en">
  <head>
    <meta charset="utf-8">
    <script type="text/javascript" src="https://cdnjs.cloudflare.com/ajax/
    libs/modernizr/2.6.2/modernizr.min.js"></script>
    <style type="text/css">
      .yes{color:green;}
      .no{color:red;}
      .svg-wrapper span{display:none;}
      .svg .yes{display:inline;}
      .no-svg .no{display:inline;}
    </style>

  </head>
  <body>

    <div class="svg-wrapper">
      <span class="yes">Huzzah!  You have SVG support.</span>
      <span class="no">BOO!  You don't have SVG support.</span>
    </div>

  </body>
</html>
```

Both spans are given the display:none rule to hide both.

On page load, Modernizr adds its feature-detection classes to the html tag. If Modernizr detects that SVG is supported, it'll add the svg class to the html tag. At that point, this span will have the display:inline rule.

Modernizr detects that SVG isn't supported, the html tag gets the no-svg class, and this span is visible.

If you test this in a browser that supports SVG, you'll see the message "Huzzah! You have SVG support." If you have a browser that doesn't support SVG, you'll see the message saying "BOO! You don't have SVG support." (You can find this example in the chapter's source code under the 8.1 directory.)

This example is rudimentary, but it displays the core idea of using Modernizr to fix cross-browser issues. Modernizr adds the classes to the `html` tag, offering a way to override styles based on Modernizr's feature detection. If you were implementing this same fix using the old user-agent method, you'd need a stylesheet for each browser that didn't support SVG, and you'd need to change the CSS for each one (for anyone interested, the only major browsers lacking SVG support are Internet Explorer 8 and under).

By adding the `svg/no-svg` class to the HTML on the page, your CSS now has a selector that can be used to override existing CSS rules. Because it's on the parent-most tag, it can be used to override other classes on the page. In this example, both span tags are given `display:none`, and if there's no SVG support, the `display:inline` declaration on the span tag with a class of `no` overrides the `display:hidden`, thanks to the `no-svg` rule on the `html` tag.

Let's try a more useful example of the same idea. You might want to have an SVG background image on the page that falls back to a PNG if the browser doesn't support SVG. By default, you'll use the PNG image. This way the SVG isn't served unless it's needed and becomes a progressive enhancement. (This example is available in the 8.2 directory.)

```
<!doctype html>
<html class="no-js" lang="en">
  <head>
    <meta charset="utf-8">
    <script type="text/javascript" src="//cdnjs.cloudflare.com/ajax/libs/
     modernizr/2.6.2/modernizr.min.js"></script>
    <style type="text/css">

      .skull{
        width:300px;
        height:300px;
        background-image:url(images/skull.png);
        background-size:100% auto;
        background-repeat: no-repeat;
      }

      .svg .skull{background-image:url(images/skull.svg);}

    </style>

  </head>
  <body>

    <div class="skull"></div>

  </body>
</html>
```

Declare the background image to use by default in the skull rule, a PNG base image.

Property declarations give size to the skull rule.

This rule will only be executed when SVG is supported. In this scenario, Modernizr will add an svg class in the html tag and the rule will be executed (see figure 8.2).

Now you have an awesome SVG skull that will look crisp for users with high-resolution displays, and will still look good for users with older browsers. Modernizr provides cross-browser capability without you having to remember or maintain a list of which browsers support SVG.

This approach is excellent for supporting features with CSS, but what about testing a user's capabilities and offering deeper support for progressive enhancements? For that, you need to take advantage of some of Modernizr's other capabilities.

8.3 JavaScript feature detection with Modernizr

A CSS hook that allows you to alter the design of a page based on which features a browser supports is a pretty handy feature, and it justifies the use of Modernizr in almost every project I work on. Ultimately, though, this leads to a bit of site bloat as you add progressive enhancements. In many cases, site functionality and interaction might also need to be progressively enhanced, and JavaScript is the best way to do that.

As I mentioned earlier, in addition to applying a series of classes to the html tag on the page, Modernizer creates a JavaScript object with Boolean values for each of the tests it runs. To check the values of the JavaScript object, it requires some base level of JavaScript ability, but it's deeply rewarding and can offer a huge degree of control over what your page loads.

If you have the example page open (directory 8.2 in this chapter's source code), open your browser's console and type Modernizr. This will return the full object in your browser with all of the tests run and each of their corresponding true or false values.

You can check these Boolean values easily by using a simple JavaScript if statement that evaluates the properties of the Modernizr JavaScript object with dot notation. In the same example page, try adding the following in the head tag:

```
<script type="text/javascript">
  if(Modernizr.opacity) {
    alert('opacity is supported');
  }
</script>
```

Reload the page, and if your browser supports CSS opacity, you'll get an alert saying "opacity is supported." This is a common CSS property, so let's try using a sensor that's more relevant to our responsive goals—touch.

8.3.1 Detecting touch support

With responsive sites, it's often not enough to detect the viewport size. You may find that sites will assume that a smaller viewport means you have touch-screen capabilities. This isn't always the case. Often I'll find myself browsing in a smaller window (say, to hide my personal browsing from my coworkers' prying eyes).

If I come across a page that assumes I have a touch screen, some elements on the page might be hidden behind touch-based systems. Or I might be on a desktop computer that has a touch interface as its primary pointer. In this case, I might have trouble tapping small links on a page designed for mouse use. It would be nice to get feedback for these use cases, and Modernizr's touch property gives you that.

Try replacing the previous opacity script example with the following:

```
<script type="text/javascript">
  if(Modernizr.touch) {
    alert('touch is supported');
  }
</script>
```

If you refresh the page on a machine that doesn't have touch support, nothing happens. Where did the alert go? The `if` statement returned `false`, so the alert contained within it wasn't run because the device does not support touch.

If you write an `else` statement after the `if`, you can run a command in the event that the `if` statement fails:

```
if(Modernizr.touch) {
    alert('touch is supported');
  }else{
    alert('touch is not supported');
  }
```

This way, your bases are covered.

Obviously, simply alerting the user to whether touch events are available isn't terribly useful. It's great for testing, but useless outside of that. What would really be helpful is if we could load one JavaScript plugin or CSS file if the test passes, and another if the test fails. Luckily Modernizr has built in a resource loader called yepnope to support this ability, and it lets you load only the scripts your user needs.

8.3.2 *Using Modernizr.load and yepnope*

Another of the advantageous features of Modernizr is yepnope, its resource loader. Using Modernizr.load, you can load a set of files depending on whether or not a test passes. This is great, because it allows you to load only the assets you need for the user visiting the website.

Yepnope (http://yepnopejs.com/) was built by the Modernizr team and is incorporated into Modernizr by default, but it has since been released as a standalone plugin, so if you need to conditionally load resources in a standalone project without Modernizr, you can.

The syntax is completely straightforward and written in plain English. Here's an example of a simple test:

```
<script type="text/javascript">
    Modernizr.load({                             Choose test you want to run.
        test: Modernizr.touch,
        yep: 'stylesheets/touch.css',
        nope: 'stylesheets/no-touch.css'
    });
</script>
```

In yep, offer files to serve if test passes.

In nope, offer files to serve if test fails.

Let's break this down a little bit. Modernizr.load runs on page load and runs the tests specified. If a test passes, the assets after `yep` are loaded. If a test fails, the assets after nope are loaded. If you run this example on a computer without touch support, `stylesheets/no-touch.css` is loaded. If the browser does have touch support, `stylesheets/touch.css` is loaded.

You can specify multiple files by enclosing the assets in brackets, like this:

```
Modernizr.load({
        test: Modernizr.touch,
        yep: ['stylesheets/touch.css', 'touch.js'],
        nope: ['stylesheets/no-touch.css', 'no-touch.js']
});
```

You can also run multiple sets of tests by passing in a JavaScript array with all your tests, like this:

```
<script type="text/javascript">
    Modernizr.load([
      {
        test: Modernizr.touch,
        yep: ['stylesheets/touch.css', 'touch.js'],
        nope: ['stylesheets/no-touch.css', 'no-touch.js']
      },
      {
        test: Modernizr.opacity,
        yep: ['stylesheets/opacity.css', 'opacity.js'],
        nope: ['stylesheets/no-opacity.css', 'no-opacity.js']
      },
      ]);
    </script>
```

This approach has a big downside in that it makes it impossible to concatenate all JavaScript files into a single JavaScript file, or all CSS files into a single CSS file. But the cost of taking this approach is offset to a large degree by the asynchronous nature of yepnope's resource loading. It's worth being aware of this downside, though, and using these features strategically.

As I'm sure you're quickly noticing, you can customize a great deal of a user's experience with Modernizr. It gives you the ability to fine-tune a website specifically for the user's needs, but what if you need to do a specific test that isn't included in the 40 or so tests included out of the box with Modernizr? Luckily, there's an easy way to add a test to Modernizr with just a little bit of JavaScript.

8.3.3 Creating custom Modernizr tests

With the ability to add a test to Modernizr, you can diversify what the plug-in is capable of and expand on its built-in capabilities. The ability to add a JavaScript object, use a CSS class, and conditionally load assets can all be ported over to custom tests. The custom test becomes fully accessible within Modernizr and operates exactly like the built-in tests.

Custom tests are added using the `addTest` method as follows:

```
Modernizr.addTest(string, function);
```

Modernizr's `addTest` function receives two parameters: the first one is a string with the name of the CSS class that you'll use to identify your test, and the second is the callback function that you'll use to test the device. The function needs to return a `true` or `false` value.

For example, if you wanted to test whether it was before 7 pm for a user, you could start with this:

```
Modernizr.addTest('night', function(){
    return true;
    });
```

In this case, the if statement, `if(Modernizr.night)`, will always be `true` and the `night` class will always be on the `head` tag. You need a function to determine if it actually is after 7 pm.

To do that, you can grab the time from the user's internal clock with some JavaScript and return the Boolean value based on that:

```
Modernizr.addTest('night', function(){        Creates new Date object
    var current = new Date();                  with current system time
    current = current.getHours();
    return !!(current >= 19)
});
```

Sets variable to current hour, based on a 24-hour clock

Returns true or false value from expression in parentheses

In this simple example we've added something incredibly helpful. This test would allow you to serve varied content based on the time of day.

8.4   Adding Modernizr to our site

Now that you understand what Modernizr is and a little bit of what it does, let's add it to the blog site we've been working on. As mentioned, adding Modernizr is as simple as linking to the source in the `head` tag and adding the `no-js` class to the `html` tag. The source code with Modernizr installed is in the 8.5 directory.

If you look at line 2 in the source code, you'll find this:

```
<html class="no-js">
```

But if you inspect the rendered HTML in the browser, you'll see that the set of Modernizr classes has been added to the `html` tag. This means Modernizr is working! Now, you may recall that in the previous chapter we added SVG graphics to the page (on line 66 of index.html in the 8.6 directory). Let's create a fallback for the SVG graphic using Modernizr.

We'll start by adding a wrapper `div` with the class of `star-svg` around the `object` tag. This will give us something to target above the SVG itself. Additionally, we can add an `img` tag linking to a PNG file for older browsers (the output of which is seen in figure 8.3):

```
<div class="star-svg">
    <object type="image/svg" width="400" height="400" style="float:right"
    data="images/star.svg">
```

```
      </object>
      <img src="images/star.png">
</div>
```

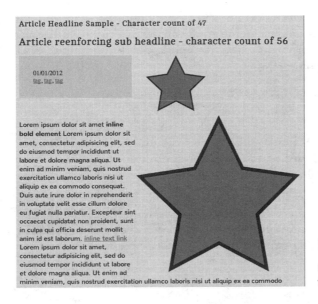

Figure 8.3 We now have two images, the SVG and the fallback PNG.

We need to add some CSS to hide and show the fallback image. On line 209 of style.css, you'll see the following:

```
.svg .star-svg img{display:none;}
.no-svg .star-svg object{display:none;}
```

That produces the results seen in figure 8.4.

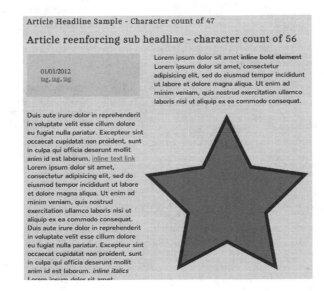

Figure 8.4 With CSS, we've hidden the second star.

In theory, this does a good job of providing a fallback for the SVG, but it has some faults. Notably, the SVG is still loaded in older browsers, and the PNG is also loaded in newer browsers.

We could circumvent some of this by using the default fallback SVG technique, in which we'd embed the fallback image within the object tag. This has the added benefit of not requiring Modernizr, and it would support graceful degradation. That would look something like this in practice:

```
<object type="image/svg+xml" data="images/star.svg">
    <img src="images/star.png">
</object>
```

Although this will work just fine, it still requires the initial SVG to fail and then serves the PNG. What would be ideal is to only serve the file to the browsers that need it. We're going to do this by using a simple Modernizr test to determine which file to load. In order to do this flexibly, we're going to change a few things.

First we'll change the star-svg class to an ID, so we can easily target it with Java-Script. We'll also use an HTML5 custom data attribute to give us the path to the asset we want to load. This attribute, titled data-path, will be the path to the directory containing both the PNG and SVG images:

```
<div id="star-svg" data-path="images/star"></div>
```

Next we'll add a conditional statement to append the extension to the filename. This conditional will use the modernizr.svg test, and if it passes, it'll create either an image tag or an SVG object depending on browser support. The final version of this code can be found in the 8.7 directory:

```
<script type="text/javascript">
  var path = $("#star-svg").attr("data-path")
  var svgObj;

    if(Modernizr.svg){
 svgObj = "<object type=\"image/svg+xml\"  style=\"float:right\" data=\""+
     path +".svg\"></object>"
    }else{
      svgObj = "<img src=\""+ path +".png\">"
    }

    $("#star-svg").html(svgObj);

</script>
```

Next, assign an empty variable, svgObj.

First, get the value of the data-path attribute.

In the test, create the full object to append with the path inserted in the variable.

The alternative string, with a traditional image tag and path to the PNG version of the image.

Here the svjObj variable is inserted within the star-svg element.

8.5   Summary

In this chapter we discussed obsolescence control, focusing on the methodologies of progressive enhancement and graceful degradation. We discussed how they're applied and outlined their differences. Hopefully, this gave you an understanding of the basics of using obsolescence control in responsive web design.

We also discussed Modernizr, which functions exceptionally well as a system with which to serve your user the required assets for their browser and create speedy and highly functional websites. Take some time and read up on Modernizr's documentation at http://modernizr.com. I've found it to be an incredibly helpful resource in my personal workflow.

Modernizr is a great tool for controlling obsolescence in websites, but to dig deep into a site's quirks, you need to learn how to test a site's performance. In order to really get under the hood of your website, you need some tools that show you what's going on behind the scenes. In the next chapter we'll discuss some tools you can use to optimize site performance in a responsive world.

8.6   *Discussion points*

- What are some of the advantages and disadvantages of progressive enhancement? What about graceful degradation?
- How can you build controls for supporting older browsers into your site designs?
- Can you think of any creative ways to use Modernizr's `addTest` method?

Testing and optimization
for responsive websites

This chapter covers

- Responsive testing
- Why optimization is crucial to building responsive experiences
- Using web inspectors to improve site performance
- Tips on improving performance

So far we've used HTML and CSS to build a responsive website that adapts to changing viewports. We've discussed how to add images and media to a responsive site and how to prevent failure in older browsers. All of this has added a lot of extra work for both designers and developers. For developers, the endeavor can be greater because achieving responsiveness in sites involves adding extra content and functionality to pages, and this introduces one of the biggest challenges of responsive web development: how to add the functionality of responsiveness without bloating the site's load time. If you add a few CSS techniques to your workflow and create pages that scale down, you've succeeded in making your websites visually scale, but potentially at the cost of performance.

One of the biggest cons people cite against responsive design is that responsive sites perform slowly, and it's true. Generally, creating responsive websites means adding responsiveness like a feature, and sometimes this means loading extra images or hiding elements. But there are some small steps you can take to ensure that your site performs optimally.

If a chair is pleasing to the eye but gives people back pain, what good is the chair? In the same way, if a responsive site is beautiful and scales nicely but comes at the expense of load time, what good is the site? The advances in hardware emulation and testing tools for both desktop and mobile devices mean it's now easier than ever to make an incredibly fast website. In previous chapters you built sites using a resized browser window. This works fine when you're only concerned with the basic scaling and architecture of a site, but there's no substitute for working directly on a device. By testing on a device, you can see exactly what the user will end up with in terms of application responsiveness, bandwidth speed and latency, and human interaction in the touch experience.

In the previous chapter, we discussed using Modernizr in progressive enhancement. In order to enact progressive enhancements, though, you have to test in order to find areas to enhance. Testing in native environments is the best way to anticipate the experience your users will have.

9.1   What is responsive testing?

Responsive web design requires a workflow that involves testing during the build process. In building a site and progressively enhancing it into the final product, you need to ensure that the site is responsive not just in size and layout, but also in its capabilities and features.

In responsive web design, it's important to remember that there's more to being responsive than anticipating browser width. The only way to get a sense of how a site works in various devices is to experience it first-hand. Most developers can't justify the expense of building their own browser labs, but there are a number of environment simulators that are available for use.

I find it's best to draft a testing plan based on a single set of devices that serve as a starting point, and to add progressive enhancements through various devices, operating systems, and environments.

9.1.1   Simulated testing environments

Simulated environments are the easiest way to test your website on various operating systems, and there are a number of software simulators available. These are simple emulators built to test operating systems outside of their native environments.

There are a few programs for Macs that simulate Windows and Android environments, as well as iOS. Unfortunately, because of Apple's software philosophy, OS X is unavailable for emulation in environments outside of Apple hardware, whereas Windows and Android environments are easily emulated within a Mac environment. This is one of the reasons why OS X is my preferred development environment.

One application that can assist in running simulated environments on Macs is Parallels (www.parallels.com/); it requires a license that costs around $80 USD. Parallels allows you to build simulated environments based on operating system and hardware standards that you set.

USING PARALLELS FOR MAC

When you first start up Parallels, you're greeted with an installation wizard that walks you through the process of setting up a new virtual machine. You're given a series of options, as shown in figure 9.1. You can install a new copy of Windows, migrate an existing copy of Windows, download Chrome OS, Ubuntu, or Android, or build a virtual machine from an OS X recovery disc.

Once it's installed, Parallels will run with your desired operating system in its own window. This window will function like an OS inside of your OS (see figure 9.2). You can share assets and test against your local host as well as anything online.

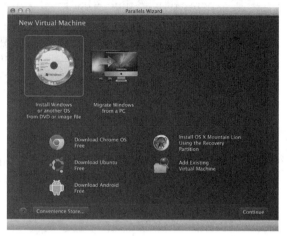

Figure 9.1 On launch, Parallels gives you options for configuring your virtual environment.

Figure 9.2 Running Windows 8 on a Mac. With this setup, I have access to a simulated environment for most web users. IE10 has the developer tools to allow you to test previous versions of IE, so the bulk of cross-browser bugs can be identified.

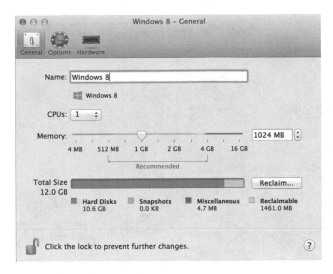

Figure 9.3 The Parallels settings for my Windows 8 virtual machine, located under Virtual Machine > Configure. Here I can reduce the amount of memory devoted to the virtual machine. In the Hardware section there's also an option to limit video memory, which is helpful in debugging animations.

The settings for each virtual machine are configurable and give you a chance to simulate variations in your testing environment (see figure 9.3). This allows you to intentionally cripple your website to see how it looks on older computers, so you can make sure you've accommodated those users. While this might seem over the top, it's incredibly helpful.

THE PROS OF PARALLELS

There are a lot of benefits to using Parallels. It's efficient and consistent, and because it's a commercial program, it has a lot of support and premium features. It lets you set up almost any configuration and combination that you might want. The simulated environments it offers give you insight into various browsers and can help identify potential problem areas before they get too serious.

THE CONS OF PARALLELS

In spite of all that Parallels can do, there are a few obvious drawbacks. First is the price tag. Apart from its own cost, using Parallels to run Windows still requires a copy of Windows, which when purchased alone is around $90 USD for the pro pack. Parallels also can be resource intensive, but no more so than a lot of other virtual machines.

There's a free alternative to Parallels released by Oracle called VirtualBox (https://www.virtualbox.org/), which gives you the same ability to install virtual machines, but it's slightly more cumbersome and I've had a lot of issues with it. It also lacks support for Chrome OS and Android. That being said, it works in a pinch.

INSTALLING IOS VIRTUAL ENVIRONMENTS

Aside from Parallels, you can simulate iOS environments in OS X using the iOS Simulator included in Xcode. Xcode is an IDE, compiler, and SDK kit for iOS development, but it also includes a set of simulators that are handy for web testing. Xcode can be

Figure 9.4   The Xcode welcome screen

downloaded for free from the App Store and installed with a click of the Install button (see figure 9.4).

To access the iPhone simulator, start up Xcode, and select Xcode > Open Developer Tools > iOS Simulator. This will give you a functioning local version of iOS that you can use to test your sites in Mobile Safari (see figure 9.5).

The simulator is very useful, but it's important to note that while this will give you a good sense of the layout and overall look and feel of your site, you'll still be lacking the native feel of touch interactions.

The iOS simulator allows you to test using a variety of iOS devices and iOS versions. You can test on any iOS version that you can install locally, and Apple provides emulators for iPhones and iPads dating back to the first models. Because Apple controls the hardware in those devices, it's easy for Apple to accurately emulate their performance.

9.2   *Browser tools for testing*

When you begin developing responsive sites, building a device lab will make for an incredible testing lab, if you can afford it. Specific devices are hard to recommend because they're constantly changing, but it's a good idea

Figure 9.5   The iOS Simulator screen. This application is incredibly useful for testing responsive websites in a simulated iOS environment.

to have a device for each major OS. Ideally, a device lab should include the following:

- A high-end Android
- A low-end Android

- An older iPhone or iPod touch
- An up-to-date iPhone or iPod touch
- A Windows phone
- An iPad
- An Android tablet

It's a good idea to spread out the screen sizes as much as possible.

Generally a spread of four or five phones and two or three tablets, each with a different OS, is a good selection. Don't worry about buying the latest device models, since they're strictly for testing, and having older devices forces you to work within tighter parameters. A site built to work well on an older phone with a slow connection will perform even better on a newer, faster phone.

In a pinch, there are also a number of emulators available for testing (discussed previously in section 9.1.1). These can show you how the software will render the page, and they're great for testing for software errors, but nothing compares to the actual experience of interacting with a website on a particular device. You can easily debug most issues for mobile and tablet devices on a simulator, but the ability to interact with a site on a physical device offers unique insight.

An easy way to get this insight is by taking a field trip to the nearest electronics store and viewing a staging environment there. This approach means you'll need a publically available testing environment, and you might have to fend off a salesperson or two, but you might learn a little about how your site operates under various conditions.

9.3   *Using web inspectors*

A web inspector is a browser tool that allows you to view the page source and the live DOM hierarchy, debug scripts, profile CPU and memory usage, view network traffic, and more. In mobile, tablet, and desktop browsers, there are a variety of inspectors available to you. Earlier we used the Chrome inspector to investigate a page's markup and CSS. As I've gotten more adept at writing code, I've found the web inspector to be one of the most important tools in my toolkit.

Internet Explorer has had a developer toolkit available since IE6. Safari has its own web inspector in both OS X and iPad. Likewise, Firefox has had a Firebug plugin available for a few years and has recently included its own developer toolset. These toolsets are much like the Chrome developer tools, but for the purposes of this book, I'm going to stick with the Chrome tools.

Aside from displaying the markup and providing a JavaScript console, the inspector lets you view how a site loads, what it loads, and how quickly it loads. In Chrome, Google even offers a plugin called PageSpeed that can test your page and help you find problem areas in your site, such as browser caching, JavaScript execution, and asset minification.

Yahoo has a similar web page performance analyzer called YSlow (https://developer.yahoo.com/yslow/), which grades your page based on a set of default rules proposed by YSlow, or by using a custom ruleset, like Google PageSpeed. YSlow is provided as a browser plugin for Firefox, Chrome, Opera, and Safari, and it can also be executed from the command line using Node.js.

9.3.1 *Mastering web inspectors*

The key to mastering web inspectors is knowing what each of the tabs at the top does and how to use it. In this section we'll cover some of the most useful features of the web inspector for Google Chrome, called Chrome DevTools:

- *Elements*—This gives you a full view of the rendered DOM and the ability to inspect each object's associated CSS as well as its DOM properties and associated event listeners. This is incredible for tweaking designs and getting feedback on potential CSS bugs. It's the default Chrome DevTools panel and the one I use most often.
- *Resources*—This panel shows the resources being used by a page, including JavaScript, CSS, and HTML, as well as the storage methods used by the browser, such as local storage and cookies.
- *Network*—In this panel you can view what's loaded, how it's applied, and its overall effect in page rendering. It will show a timeline of how the page loads. You can even break down to the millisecond how various assets affect the page load.
- *Sources*—This panel is used for debugging JavaScript and CSS and can help you track down the root issues in JavaScript applications.
- *Timeline*—In this panel you can record a page load and dive deep into how the page is loading and how the load time is affected.
- *Console*—This panel is useful for viewing and testing JavaScript objects, and it's also great for logging messages when debugging.

Two of these panels, Resources and Network, are especially helpful in creating a responsive website. They'll help you optimize your site and reduce the user's overall bandwidth burden.

ELEMENTS

In the Elements panel you have access to the full DOM. Here you can see everything as you wrote it after it's been affected by JavaScript and even while JavaScript runs on the page. Once you select an element to inspect, you have a full view of its CSS properties, including all selectors affecting the object and their computed styles, as well as DOM properties and event listeners. We discussed the inspector in chapters 5 and 8, so there's no need to go into depth here.

RESOURCES

In the Resources panel, you can view the elements being queried by the server on page load. These are seen under Frames, and can be used to identify what CSS and JavaScript is being loaded, as well as images and other assets. If you are loading something you don't need, or there are places where you can be more efficient, this will quickly become apparent.

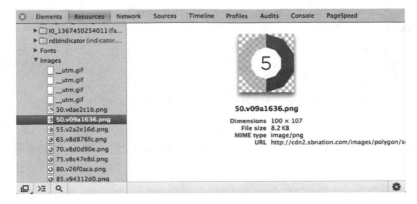

Figure 9.6   Inspecting an image in the Resources panel

When you click on an asset, you can view what the source is and see its size in terms of data type, size, and dimensions, as shown in figure 9.6. This gives you a sense of every element's weight in the load process.

NETWORK

The Network panel is of particular interest when you're trying to optimize a site's efficiency for responsive websites. This tool will help you get a visual sense of every request and its effects on your site's load time, because it shows the request a page makes and the time it takes to execute that request (see figure 9.7).

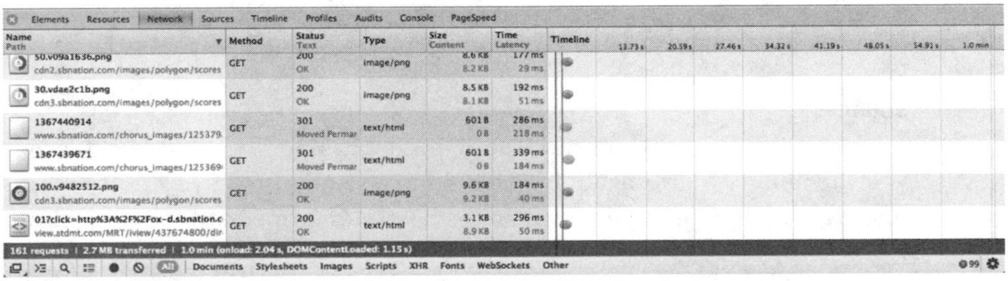

Figure 9.7   The Network panel

A client (or web browser) makes a request for every asset used on the page, and then a server sends a response. After this handshake between the client and the server, the page can begin to load. This means every image file, CSS file, and JavaScript file requires a request to a server (if the file wasn't previously loaded and cached by the browser). These requests take time, called the *round-trip time* (RTT).

> **CLIENT-SERVER HANDSHAKE**   The client-server handshake actually breaks down into three round trips from the client to the server: the first to find the file (called *DNS name resolution*), the second to establish a TCP connection, and the third to begin transferring the file.

Accessing developer tools on iOS

In iOS 6, Apple began including the ability to access Safari's developer tools within the desktop version of Safari from an iPhone or iPad. This gives you the ability to inspect elements on your iPhone.

To do this, attach your iPhone or iPad to a Mac with the USB cord and then open Safari. Once there, you can access the developer tools on Safari by clicking Develop > Devices from the toolbar and selecting your device. The window you'll see is similar to the Chrome developer tools. In figure 9.8, the Safari developer tools are running from an attached iPhone.

Figure 9.8   Safari developer tools running from an attached iPhone

SOURCES

In the Sources panel you can inspect specific source files used in the project, giving you the ability to investigate individual files (see figure 9.9). This is mostly useful in debugging JavaScript, but it can also be helpful in inspecting your CSS files.

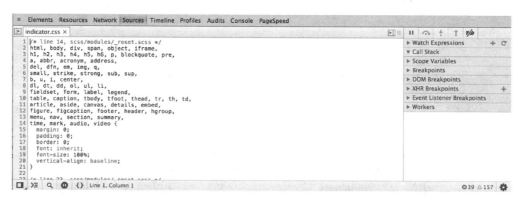

Figure 9.9   The Sources panel in Chrome developer tools

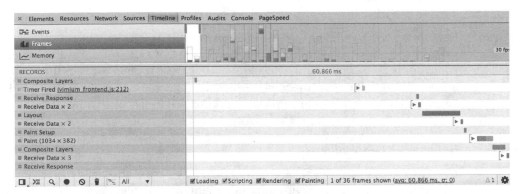

Figure 9.10   The Timeline panel displays real-time load-processing information.

The Sources tool also lets you modify the resources in memory live—you can change your CSS and JavaScript files and immediately see the changes. Be aware that those changes are made in memory, so they'll be lost when the page is reloaded.

TIMELINE

The Timeline panel gives you the opportunity to see the loading of a page on a microscopic level. This gives you a visual representation of all the requests made on page load, the time taken to return those requests, and the assets' total load time (see figure 9.10).

When you're trying to reduce total load time, it's important to look first at the number of requests being made and see if there are any ways to reduce them. You can also investigate whether any files are taking an extraordinary amount of time to load.

It's also important to remember the load order of a page. Pages start with the initial DOM load and then load CSS; at that point, the page is displayed and JavaScript is executed. In the timeline, you can watch how your page loads all of these assets.

The timeline will show loading, scripting, rendering, and painting of the page in real time once you click the Record button. The recording can be stopped to analyze the results, and you can zoom in on different parts of the process to get in-depth feedback.

CONSOLE

In the Console panel you get to interact with the site's JavaScript. We've used the Console in previous chapters to log screen size and get easy access to the pixel width of the page on load. Aside from getting diagnostic information, you can use the Console as a live shell prompt for JavaScript. You can interact with page elements and JavaScript objects.

The Console is hugely helpful in interacting with JavaScript APIs because it can return and log values, giving you the opportunity to see a visual readout of results being returned. The ability to use a shell prompt also affords you the opportunity to run functions and see their effects live on the page. The Console is hugely helpful in debugging JavaScript.

9.4   *Tips on reducing request times*

Despite increasing bandwidth, HTTP requests still create a latency problem in a majority of sites because they're highly dependent on both the user and the server. This is particularly an issue in mobile development because mobile users in the United States are often on cellular connections, which tend to be slower than Wi-Fi and feature bandwidth caps. The server requests need to be reduced, and assets being transferred need to be minified to improve performance.

9.4.1   *Reducing HTTP requests*

Reducing HTTP requests is of major importance across all sites, but it's not just load time that's a concern. Most users are impatient when first experiencing a new site, and if the site doesn't load in a matter of seconds, the user will leave. The initial HTTP requests can add to the time before the site begins rendering, increasing the number of people who leave before the site has loaded. Reducing these initial requests can give you a dramatic advantage over your competition. There's also more and more information coming out about the effect of load time on search-engine optimization.

Every DNS lookup a browser does comes at a cost to the total load time, so the fewer servers that are involved, the fewer lookups are necessary. There's a strategy to using a second or third domain in order to run parallel downloads, which we'll talk about in section 9.4.3.

Another big way to improve performance is to ensure that there are no bad requests on your page. These are wasteful and can bog the site down as an asset searches for a nonexistent asset. This problem is much more common than most people think. Sometimes it's the result of trying to pull in an old JavaScript file that no longer exists in the head tag; other times it's a bad path to a rarely used image in a CSS file. It's important to ensure that on every page load, the page can find all the required assets. This means making sure you write correct paths to assets, and that you maintain those paths in the live environment.

Once you've minimized the page's requests, it's time to start tending to your site's assets. Minifying JavaScript and CSS is one excellent way to do that, and it's well-covered territory. The YUI Compressor from the Yahoo Developer team is a great resource for JavaScript and CSS compression (http://yui.github.io/yuicompressor/). Image compression is another big one; I use ImageOptim (https://imageoptim.com/).

Developer insight: compressing CSS and JS

Compressing CSS and JavaScript files can save a lot of extra bytes, but sometimes it can cause legacy issues for future developers who might not know what compression technique is being implemented. When compressing files, make sure you document how you compressed the assets so anyone else working on the project knows how to make changes on the original JavaScript and CSS files and compress them again for production. It's also a good practice to keep production-ready compressed files separate from uncompressed development files to reduce confusion.

9.4.2 Reducing image requests with Base64 encoding

Images are another major focus when improving site performance. There are applications to help you compress images and reduce their overall burden on the site. One way to optimize images is to use *Base64 encoding*. This means breaking down an image into its data form and inserting it into your CSS that way. Base64 encoding will increase total image size by about 33%, but it can reduce a file request in exchange.

I find this method to be extremely effective for textures on a site; you can easily save yourself some HTTP requests by including the texture as a Base64 image. The amount of data will be slightly larger, but you'll spare yourself a request by including the image in the CSS. Base64-encoding images in your CSS is more about saving the request for the image than it is about saving file size.

You can convert an image into Base64 by using any number of tools online, like the one from the Web Coder Tools site (http://webcodertools.com/imagetobase 64converter/). A quick search will identify several sites that offer such services. Once you have the string that represents the image, you can easily insert it into your CSS with the following code:

```
body {
  background-image: url(data:image/png;base64,
    [ long string of Base64 data here ]
  );
}
```

This may seem completely foreign and complicated, but it works exactly like a normal background image. Use this technique sparingly and only for small images of just a few KB.

9.4.3 Speed optimization check list

One of the companies that's an absolute trailblazer in the optimization and page-speed category is Yahoo. An alternative to Page Speed by Google is Yahoo's YSlow, which we touched on earlier. Yahoo has even publicized a list of 35 best-practice categories, available online at https://developer.yahoo.com/performance/rules.html.

In keeping with this excellent checklist, here are some of the rules presented in Yahoo's best practices and some ways to optimize against each rule:

- *Minimize HTTP requests.* As discussed earlier, minimizing requests can boost site performance exponentially. Combining all JavaScript files into a single script or all CSS into a single stylesheet is a great way to improve response times. Using CSS sprites (as mentioned in chapter 6) is another way to optimize image loading.
- *Use a content delivery network.* A content delivery network, or CDN, is a series of web servers with the dedicated purpose of serving static files across multiple locations. Each user is served the assets based on network location, reducing the number of network hops in order to receive an asset. There are multiple services providing low-cost CDNs, such as Akamai and Amazon. A CDN is best used for static content, but it's one of the best ways to improve site performance.

- *Put stylesheets at the top.* Putting stylesheets in the head tag of a page ensures that a page loads progressively, meaning that content at the top of the page loads before content at the bottom of the page. This gives the user visual feedback about the page-load progress and serves as an indicator of overall page load. While it won't do anything magical to reduce page size, it will give the page the appearance of a fast load, creating a more satisfying user experience.

- *Put scripts at the bottom.* JavaScript blocks parallel loading of page assets. This means the order of script tags as they appear on the DOM is the order in which they are downloaded and then executed. In order to ensure that a page renders visually as quickly as possible, it's best to put script tags at the bottom of the page. This allows the page to load its visual elements first, and then to execute any functional JavaScript.

- *Split components across multiple domains.* This works in conjunction with establishing a CDN, but by putting assets on different domains, you can maximize parallel downloads. You should avoid using more than two or three domains, but hosting static content on parallel CDN domains will ensure rapid delivery and parallel loading of those assets.

- *Keep components under 25 KB.* Keeping site components under 25 KB is important to making site assets cacheable in iPhones. The iPhone has a 25 KB cache limit and won't store files larger than 25 KB uncompressed.

- *Avoid empty image* src *attributes.* Images with empty src attributes—for example, <img src="">—cause major page-rendering issues. In short, the browser spends a lot of time looking for an asset that isn't there, and this blocks the rendering of other page assets.

The full list of page-speed best practices can be found in the performance section of Yahoo's developer portal (https://developer.yahoo.com/performance/rules.html).

9.5   Summary

In this chapter, we discussed the importance of site optimization in responsive web design. You learned how to use web inspectors to view the document structure and discover valuable information about how your page loads and what assets are being used. In this chapter we learned the tools of the trade needed to optimize your responsive websites.

By optimizing for performance, you can regulate any additional assets you might develop in building a responsive website, like feature-detection libraries, additional images, and viewport-specific code. Performance is absolutely crucial to responsive design because sites need to run on such a wide array of devices with variations in their capabilities.

We also covered a few less common tips on how to optimize page loads and reduce server requests. By optimizing your pages, you can reduce page load time even after adding the additional code needed to create a responsive website, and you'll ensure that your pages work well within the constraints of mobile.

9.6   *Discussion points*

- How can you consider performance optimizations when beginning the development process?
- How can design contribute to a site's performance?
- What are some ways you can easily examine site performance?

appendix A
Context-aware design

This appendix covers

- Introducing context awareness in web design
- Level-four media queries
- Using JavaScript for context awareness

This book provides an introduction to the concept of responsive web design. Hopefully after reading it you'll understand how to design and develop responsive websites. As has been mentioned, responsive web design means providing your users with a layout that adapts to their needs. Responsive web design illustrates a primitive form of context-aware computing.

What if, instead of resizing the design to adapt to the user's device, you could also format parts of the site based on factors like location, time of day, the user's history on the site, or the user's activity level. Theoretically, all of this data is accessible to the design of a page and could be used to greatly enhance the user's experience.

By implementing some forms of context awareness in websites, you could streamline the interface options. For example, you could use context awareness to make assumptions about why a visitor is visiting the page, such as for a user who often visits a site for specific reasons. Perhaps you run a site that provides weather information. In this case, knowing the user's location would give you the opportunity to serve them the weather in their area.

I recently discussed this topic with a colleague who runs a website for a creamery. He told me that he used IP address and time of day to serve content that was immediately relevant to the user. If it was spring or summer, the website would promote ice cream. If you were on an IP address close to the creamery itself, it would show you how close the creamery is.

While this practice holds a lot of potential for web design, context awareness has long been a practice in native application development.

A.1   *Context awareness in applications*

In native apps, specifically in mobile devices, context awareness is common. When the iPhone first launched, it solved a common problem in smartphone use through a little insight into context awareness. Prior to the iPhone, smartphones suffered from not knowing how a user was using the phone. If you had the phone to your head, sometimes the screen would remain on. This was solved by the inclusion of a proximity sensor in the iPhone, which would disable the screen as you raised it to your face. With this minor element of context awareness, the utility and battery life of the phone was greatly increased.

In apps like Yelp and Foursquare, where geographic location can play an important part in what the application does, context awareness is fundamental to how the app works. In iOS development the Core Location framework gives the application locational awareness to native applications. By using location data, applications can automatically serve location-specific content. In the case of apps like Yelp, this data can be the locations of nearby restaurants or shops.

In addition to offering GPS-based location management in iOS, the iPhone 5S introduced a new co-processor, the M7. The M7 offers iOS applications the ability to track motion-related activity by combining information from the accelerometer, gyroscope, and compass. This information is available through the Core Motion framework. In an iOS 7 application, developers can access whether the user is standing still, walking, running, or driving. By giving developers access to the user's activity, a design can prioritize around that activity.

By accessing the user's active state, you can augment the UI to make buttons and images bigger if the user is walking, or to disable distracting features while the user is driving. A walking user might not be able to focus as closely as when they are still, so it might be in your application's best interests to increase the size of interface elements. If the user is sitting still, the user will be able to interact more precisely, so the user interface could have smaller interface elements, allowing more room for varied content.

In the near future, as wearable technology increases in popularity, it's not hard to imagine an application using a more detailed set of sensors and levels of contextual interaction. Say, for example, that a user is wearing a device that features a heart-rate monitor. If the user has an elevated heart rate, an application could route incoming unimportant phone calls directly to voicemail until the operating system observes the user's pulse returning to normal.

While context awareness might be helpful in application development, what about its utility on the web? In design, we often develop based on strict guidelines, serving a single design for all of our visitors. In simple brochure sites, or web apps with a single use, this approach might work just fine, but sometimes there's a huge benefit to using varied content in contextually relevant ways. What if you could expand the context awareness of responsive design and its principles into an awareness of where a user is and what they're doing?

A.2 *Context awareness on the web*

Web designers and developers might not have access to something as powerful as Apple's M7 co-processor in the browser, but there are things a developer can to do improve a user's experience based on contextual factors, such as time of day or geographic location.

One of the best examples I can think of is a website promoting beverages. The beverages people drink might change dramatically through the day. For example, in the morning you might want to promote a cup of coffee with a banner on your page, as in figure A.1.

Figure A.1   A banner advertising hot coffee, an ideal morning beverage

On a page, you need an h1 tag and some CSS to style it (this code can be found in the source code directory for appendix A, in folder A1.1):

```
<!doctype html>
<html lang="en">
  <head>
    <meta charset="utf-8">
    <style type="text/css">          This CSS will give the coffee message
      h1.coffee{                     its wonderful brown color.
        text-align: center;
        color:#c18230;
        background-color: #4a2b03;
      }
    </style>
  </head>
  <body>

    <h1 id="message" class="coffee">We have hot coffee!</h1>    Here's where
                                                                you'll display
  </body>                                                        your message.
</html>
```

This morning banner is great for anyone visiting your website in the early morning, but if you're anything like me, having a cup of coffee in the evening is a terrible idea.

What if your shop sells beer? That might be the perfect drink to end a long day of grinding code, so after 6 pm you could recommend a nice cold beer. For anyone visiting between those times, you could offer something more generic, like a diet soda.

In order to do this, you need to follow a few steps. First you need to access what time it is for the user of the site, and then set a few contextual breakpoints. Much like breakpoints in responsive web design, contextual breakpoints are identified points at which augmenting a site's design makes sense. While responsive design deals strictly with site layout and screen width, contextual breakpoints could involve any factor that might change how a person uses part of a site.

A.2.1 Contextual breakpoints

With   responsive web design, you change the layout of the page based on screen widths, called *breakpoints*. In contextual design, we can use this term, *breakpoints*, to discuss the places where we change context.

In order to achieve context awareness, you need to first establish some breakpoints to adjust context around. In the beverage example, you offer hot coffee in the morning, but you might also want to promote beer or diet soda at different times of the day. We've identified one factor that needs to change (the beverage being served), and one context to change it against (the time of day). The context that instigates the change will serve as our contextual breakpoint, so we can identify "6 pm" as a contextual breakpoint—that's when we change from soda to beer.

In order to better understand this, table A.1 shows when the message will change and what it will change to. You can see that there are specific times when the message changes: 4 am, 12 pm, and 6 pm. These can serve as contextual breakpoints.

Table A.1 Beverage messages at different times of day

Time	Message
4 am–12 pm	"We have hot coffee!"
12 pm–6 pm	"We have diet soda!"
6 pm–4 am	"We have cold beer!"

These time ranges give a good sense of what the context for each of the messages will be, but you also need to identify a key/value pairing so that you can implement these in your page. This will become clear in a minute when you start building some contextual tests.

In order to better interpret these breakpoints, let's give them some simple strings that you can work with in JavaScript (see table A.2). This works nicely for now, but you could also expand this out to other contextual factors.

Table A.2 Breakpoints with key/value strings

Time [breakpoint key]	Message [module value]
4 am–12 pm (morning)	"We have hot coffee!" (coffee)
12 pm–6 pm (afternoon)	"We have diet soda!" (soda)
6 pm–4 am (evening)	"We have cold beer!" (beer)

Say, for instance, that you have a baseball site. You might want to feature a specific team more prominently to visitors from particular regions. You could use a user's GPS location to determine if they're in a region that favors a specific team and serve modules for that team in prominent places on the page. A few of the contextual breakpoints might look like those in table A.3.

Table A.3 Contextual breakpoints for regions and baseball teams

Region	Team
New England	Boston Red Sox
New York State	New York Yankees
Washington DC	Washington Nationals
Missouri	Kansas City Royals
Wisconsin	Wisconsin Brewers

In table A.3 you have regions as contextual breakpoints: New England, New York State, Washington DC, Missouri, and Wisconsin.

What you need now is a way to do things differently based on whether the user meets the restrictions of the contextual breakpoints. Much like with a media query, if a browser's width is under X, some styles are served; if the width is between X and Y, other styles are served; and if the width is over Y, another set of styles is served. With context awareness, if a user meets condition A, some functions should execute and some assets should be loaded, and if they meet condition B, other functions should execute and other assets should be loaded.

Getting back to the beverage module, now that you have the contextual breakpoints in mind, you're free to alter your module. You simply need to figure out how. Establishing context is tricky, though. There's no set object to establish it against. In responsive design there's a solid value (such as viewport width), but with context awareness you need to establish something more dynamic.

In chapter 8 we discussed Modernizr, a JavaScript library for cross-browser testing. In that chapter we touched on yepnope.js, a tool that will give you everything you need to conditionally load assets. Using yepnope.js, you can load contextual assets based on passing a Boolean value. In chapter 8 we did this by passing in a Modernizr test, which returns Boolean (`true` or `false`) values. In order to use custom context awareness, you need to create your own test.

We discussed the `addTest` method in chapter 8 as well. One way to create new, custom contextual modules is by adding them to Modernizr. This will give you all the flexibility of having Modernizr style classes available within your site's CSS, but it comes at a cost: Modernizr prevents the page from loading until all tests are completed. This is important to how Modernizr works, but it may be too cumbersome for what you want to accomplish.

Instead of relying on Modernizr for this, we'll use yepnope to conditionally load assets related to the context. But first you have to write some functions to test with. In the beverage module, you want to test what time it is for the user, and based on the time, you'll use yepnope to load in some new assets and then execute a function.

A.2.2 *Creating contextual tests*

You start by creating a namespace for your contextual tests. On line 7 in the A.2 directory of the appendix A source code, you'll create a "context" object to use as a namespace for your tests. Within the namespace, you'll create functions for each of your contextual breakpoints—morning, afternoon, and evening:

```
<script type="text/javascript">
  var context = {
    morning: function(x){},
    afternoon: function(x){},
    evening: function(x){},
  };

</script>
```

Now you can access these functions as `context.morning`, `context.afternoon`, and `context.evening`.

Within each of these, you need to create functions that will return `true` or `false` based on what you want to test against. Before you do that, though, you'll add a helper function to return the current time:

```
var hours = function(){
  var current = new Date();
  current = current.getHours();
  return current;
}
```

With this, you can create your tests. You'll use the generic x parameter and the `hours()` helper function to pass the time to your contextual tests. In the context object you'll create simple conditional statements and return them directly in the functions. In the A.3 source code you can see the `hours()` function, as well as the tests returning Boolean values:

```
var hours = function(){
  var current = new Date();
```

```
    current = current.getHours();
    return current;
}

var context = {
  morning: function(x){
    return !!(x > 4 && x < 12);
  },
  afternoon: function(x){
    return !!(x >= 12 && x < 18);
  },
  evening: function(x){
    return !!(x >= 18 && x < 24 || x > 0 && x <= 4);
  },
};
```

The double exclamation points in the preceding code will directly return the results of the conditional statement as a Boolean value. With this, you have set your three conditional tests in motion.

Now you need to run a loop to test for each of your contexts and load the conditional assets for the three tests:

```
for (x in context) {
  console.log(context[x](hours()));
}
```

This code will log the results of each test as true or false. You should get two false and one true when you run this code.

Next you can create your yepnope.js loads for the tests. Yepnope.js will load Java-Script files for morning, afternoon, and evening:

```
for (x in context) {}
  yepnope([{
    test:   context[x](hours()),
    yep: "contexts/" + x + ".js",
    complete: function(){
    }
  }])
}
```

This code will conditionally load assets. Now you need to run a function to give you some CSS hooks, as in Modernizr. You can use an if statement for this:

```
if(eval(test)){
  var html = document.documentElement;
  html.className += "is-" + x;
};
```

This code will add "is-" to the name of your contextual breakpoint; in the evening, it'll produce the name "is-evening" and append "is-evening" to the HTML class on your page.

Now you can tie all of this together with some CSS.

A.2.3   *Contextual CSS*

You have a series of tests that add classes to the HTML object on the page, so now you can use some conditional CSS. The example already has the brown "We have hot coffee" message at the top of the page. Now you can add afternoon and evening messages.

First create three CSS rules for each of the contextual breakpoints—one for `is-morning`, one for `is-afternoon`, and one for `is-evening`:

```css
.is-morning h1#message{
  text-align: center;
  color:#c18230;
  background-color: #4a2b03;
}

.is-evening h1#message{
  text-align: center;
  color:#4e63cb;
  background-color: #152058;
}

.is-afternoon h1#message{
  text-align: center;
  color:#e04f28;
  background-color: #802209;
}
```

All you're doing here is changing the color of the backgrounds. If you check out your browser, you'll see a brown message in the morning, a red message in the afternoon, and a blue message in the evening (see figure A.2). The source code for this demo can be found in the A.5 directory.

Here you've styled the three messages uniquely for the contextual tests. This styling can be extended throughout the page, and any major assets you want loaded can be brought in contextually with yepnope. For example, change the text of your sample message in the contexts/morning.js file. You can start by creating a global variable called message:

```js
var message;
```

Then you can set `message` to the morning coffee message.

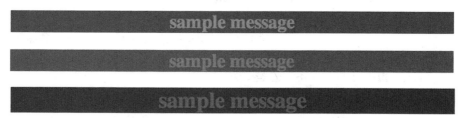

Figure A.2   The morning, afternoon, and evening styles applied to the placeholder `h1`

In the yepnope `complete` function, change the contents of the h1 on the page to display the `message`. Here's a replace-text function:

```
var replaceText = function(x){
  var module = document.getElementById("message");
  module.innerHTML = x;
};
```

You can also move all the code to the bottom of the page so it executes after the DOM is fully rendered. With this final bit of code, you have a good basic example of how a contextually aware site might work.

A.3   Summary

In this appendix you learned the basics of contextual web design. With contextually aware websites, you can improve the user's experience by serving site content based on how your users are using the site. This appendix barely scratches the surface of what's possible with context awareness.

With the concepts in this appendix, you can start introducing context awareness to your websites. You can use contextual breakpoints much like traditional responsive breakpoints. By using the "context" namespace for your tests, you can introduce a series of tests; by using yepnope, you can load conditional assets according to the test results, and then execute some JavaScript once the assets are loaded.

The demo in this appendix is simplistic, but it introduces the concepts you need to start building complex, contextually aware web designs. The depth of sites this enables you to create is nearly limitless. Using information based on a user's context can deeply enhance a user's site experience and can lead to new and innovative ways of presenting a site's user interface.

index

MORE TITLES FROM MANNING

Secrets of the JavaScript Ninja
by John Resig and Bear Bibeault

ISBN: 9781933988696
392 pages, $39.99
December 2012

Sass and Compass in Action
by Wynn Netherland, Nathan Weizenbaum,
   Chris Eppstein, and Brandon Mathis

ISBN: 9781617290145
240 pages, $44.99
July 2013

HTML5 in Action
by Rob Crowther, Joe Lennon, Ash Blue,
   and Greg Wanish

ISBN: 9781617290497
466 pages, $34.99
Febraury 2014

For ordering information go to www.manning.com